The Poverty of Nations

The Poverty of Nations

Reflections on Underdevelopment and the World Economy

Michael Manley

PLUTO PRESS
London • Concord, Mass

First published 1991 by Pluto Press
345 Archway Road, London N6 5AA
and 141 Old Bedford Road
Concord, MA 01742, USA

British Library Cataloguing in Publication Data
Manley, Michael, *1924-*
    The poverty of nations: reflections on underdevelopment
and the world economy.
    1. Developing countries. Economic development. Effects of
imperialism
    I. Title
    330.91724

    ISBN 0-7453-0314-5
    ISBN 0-7453-0449-4 pbk

Library of Congress Cataloging-in-Publication Data
Manley, Michael, 1924-
    The poverty of nations: reflections on underdevelopment
and the world economy/ Michael Manley.
        p. cm.
    Includes bibliographical references and index.
    ISBN 0-7453-0314-5. – ISBN 0-7453-0449-4 (pbk.)
    1. Developing countries. 2. Developing countries –
Economic policy. 3. Imperialism. 4. International economic
relations.
    I. Title.
    HC59.7.M283 1990
    338.9'0091724'0904–dc20   90-7613
                                                             CIP

Typeset in 11 on 13pt Stone by Stanford DTP, Milton Keynes
Printed in the United Kingdom by
Billing and Sons Ltd., Worcester

Contents

Acknowledgements

My very special thanks go to the people who have become my indispensable allies in everything that I write or plan to author.

Tony Bogues does all the research and therefore deserves whatever credit is due to scholarship.

Glynne Ewart edits everything with an eye both sensitive and relentless in its search for redundancy and appropriate structure.

I owe a special debt of gratitude to Marva Roberts who transcribed the Columbia University Lectures on which this book is based.

And of course, without the support of Pluto Press the book would never have seen the light of day!

Michael Manley
January 1991

Introduction

The decade of the 1980s was catastrophic for the Third World. Whether it was famine or the debt bondage, the dream of many Third World societies of achieving sustained development died. Translated into human terms, there was famine in Sub-Saharan Africa. In countries where there was no famine, the food situation worsened compared to the 1970s. In 1974, experts stated that the average food intake in many Third World nations was below what was medically required for reasonable health. In the 1980s it got worse. In Ghana it was 66 per cent of the minimum requirement; in Mozambique it was 71 per cent. In relation to debt, the Third World continued to be stuck in the economic morass. Many Third World countries attempted to adjust their economies structurally with International Monetary Fund remedies. Despite this, the total Third World debt grew from US$560 billion in 1980 to over $1 trillion in 1988. Simultaneously there was, by that same year, a net negative transfer of over $50 billion from the developing to developed countries. An observer would note these facts and would also note that interest payments owed annually by Latin American countries stood at over $40 billion and continues to rise. Most Third World countries were obliged to commit between one-third to two-thirds of their gross export receipts to the service of debts. In some cases this figure reached a staggering 75 per cent. In several cases the total external indebtedness of the Third World nations exceeded their gross national product (GNP).

After a pause our observer might reflect upon the fact that the level of Third World debt is explained in terms of the bias of the person who explains it. For example, commentators from the developed world commonly dismiss this debt as a result of the extravagance, the corruption, the inexperience, or even all three, of those who have administered the affairs of Third World countries since their attainment of political independence.

On the other hand, Third World commentators will not hesitate to point out that the debt is a direct and inevitable consequence of the structural imbalance in the world economy. They will point to the terms of trade which move chronically against the interests of largely commodity-exporting developing countries. They will point to protectionism among developed countries which shuts out the products of newly born Third World manufacturing industries. They will certainly direct attention to the cost of money which has risen dramatically in the last ten years.

Third World analysts will admit that there have been cases of extravagance and even corruption. They will not dispute a measure of inexperience. But they will be quick to demonstrate that these have been aberrations which pale into insignificance beside the overwhelming realities of the world economy and the way it functions.

Even as that debate rages, our observer will remark sadly that whatever the causes, the results add up to a form of collective madness. The Third World represents one-half or three-quarters of the world population depending on whether one includes China or not. This is a vast source of productive and market potential. As it lies economically stagnant, if not actually contracting, a huge potential contribution to the forward move-ment of the world economy lies paralysed.

By now there will be the temptation to give up; to surrender to a prevailing mood of futility in the face of the cupidity and short-sightedness of those who manage the dominant component of the world economy. Attention will probably turn to the danger of a nuclear holocaust. As deeper connections between the first and second areas of concern occur, it may be recalled that 1985 saw the world committing $1,000 billion to the production of weapons of destruction. More than $60 billion of this was spent on research alone in spite of the fact that the US and the USSR possess, between them, the capacity to wipe each other out ten times over.

By this stage it will not need the proddings of an observer for it to be noticed that the money spent on military research could, with prudent application, provide the means for a virtual revolution in the growth potential of Third World economies. It is in this context that the question of Third World develop-ment looms as an issue larger than the question of the fate of the peoples of the Third World alone. It is no longer seriously in dispute that there is an intimate connection between the economic fate of the former colonies and that of their former owners. But what is Third World development; what has been the experi-ence with it; one might even ask, what is development itself?

Judging by the state of affairs on a case by case basis by the mid-1980s, one would be obliged to say that Latin America and the Caribbean were at least cur-rently unsuccessful in their development programmes. Measured by just two indicators: debt and the state of unemployment, it would be impossible to claim that these two areas, comprising one geographical region, represent a success story.

Sub-Saharan Africa represents an equally dismal picture. Its debts are not as high but the capacity to repay them is that much less. Ethiopia, Somalia and the greater part of East Africa present pictures that vary between famine to the north and comparative failures of agricultural production to the south. Drought has undoubtedly been a major factor but does not tell the whole story of the inability of this region to achieve significant economic growth and raise standards of living for the majority of its people.

If one turns to the Middle and Far East, the picture, at a superficial glance, is more complicated. India has achieved great successes in both industrial and agricultural production but remains one of the poorest nations in the world judged by the test of per capita national income. Is this just the result of a continuing population explosion, or are there deeper causes? Pakistan and Bangladesh remain poor and cannot even boast India's apparent productive successes. South Korea, Taiwan and Singapore are commonly presented as success stories. Certainly, they have achieved spectacular rates of economic growth. However, several questions suggest themselves. Each has benefited from very special circumstances in terms of geopolitics. For example, not every Third World country has the strategic advantage of a communist state on its northern border and a geopolitical commitment to its success on the part of the authorities in Washington. There are further questions involving political and other freedoms that must be examined before one can accept the label 'success' without qualification. Furthermore, Puerto Rico and Jamaica, after 1980, enjoyed very special relations with Washington. Yet Puerto Rico depends upon food stamps to feed much of its population despite substantial growth. Jamaica suffered severe social reverses between 1980 and 1989. Economic growth registered in 1987 and 1988 left the country with lower gross domestic product (GDP) per capita than obtained in 1978. In addition the major productive sectors still lagged behind 1978 levels. Tourism and imports fuelled by external borrowing accounted for the positive GDP figures.

Then again, there is Cuba. Astonishing success in terms of social welfare has been achieved by the Cuban revolution which created health and education systems that begin to challenge their First World equivalents. On the other hand, the revolution cannot boast an outstanding economic success. Its detractors point to slow economic growth in spite of huge support from the Soviet Union. Its defenders point to the tremendous damage done by United States hostility and in particular the US economic embargo. Thus do the contradictions multiply the closer one looks.

The question of Third World development has attracted its fair share of cliches. The observer whom we consulted at the outset spoke of First World perceptions of extravagance, corruption and inexperience. It has become commonplace for these commentators to attribute the 'successes' of Taiwan, Singapore and South Korea to a phenomenon known as 'the Asian work ethic'. On the other hand, Third World apologists have tended to attribute the difficulties of the Third World entirely to the effects of history and the present structure of the world economy. All of this represents dangerous oversimplification. The Third World is not some homogeneous social phenomenon comprised of countries with similar economies, social structures and political experiences. Different Third World countries with similar exposures to imperialism and colonialism exhibit widely differing features today. External and internal factors interact. Both must be studied.

The first thing to be observed when looking at the Third World is the variety of attempts at development. From as far back as the 1940s there was a model of development named after Puerto Rico. This reflected the attempt by the Puerto Rican people to deal with their problems of poverty, inadequate productive capacity and largely absent social services in terms of their own experience and their own circumstances. This was later defined as the first example of a dependent capitalist path to development, so named because private capital, mostly foreign, was identified as the main engine of economic growth and because Puerto Rico was dependent upon the United States for many of its services, for its security and for its new investment capital.

Since that time, South Korea, Taiwan and Singapore have provided their own variants to this model.

Marxist/Leninist Cuba has presented a strikingly different approach to development. So too has Tanzania with its emphasis on self-reliance and co-operative agricultural organisation.

Latin America, and to some extent the English speaking Caribbean, have proceeded along lines that are similar, in some respects, to that of Puerto Rico but with marked differences. There has been more emphasis on local capital formation and production in the area of import substitution. There have been inconsistent experiments with agrarian reform and 'basic needs' strategies aimed at developing new production around the satisfaction of the fundamental need for food, clothing and housing.

There has been a lack of understanding of the relationship between three variables. First, there is the history of the world from the sixteenth to the twentieth centuries, a history that has been dominated by modern imperialism; its author: the emergence and eventual world dominance of the capitalist system; and its offspring: modern colonialism. Secondly, there is the economic, social and political structure of the different parts of the world that were conquered and colonised as imperialism spread across the world. These indigenous structures interacted with the particular form which imperialism and colonialism took in ways that were peculiar to each area. Thirdly, there is the nature of the independence struggle through which each area sought to escape from the domination of the imperial power.

There were many common factors running like threads through the historical experience in each of these variables. But there were also many factors unique to each situation and the interaction which resulted. It is the search for an understanding of the common factors, the variables and the particular interactions which led to this book.

The book will deal first with a summary of the growth of imperialism and colonialism between broadly 1600 and 1945. Mercantilism, the industrial revolution, the emergence of the capitalist system, the later evolution of finance capital and the final flowering of the transnational corporation system are traced in necessarily compressed form. They are examined for their impact upon the countries which were conquered, colonised or even 'discovered' as the system spread.

The societies that were swept up in the general expansion of the imperialist system are looked at in equally compressed form. Clues are sought as to why independence struggles took different forms with different motives under the leadership of different local interest groups.

Four development models are examined. Puerto Rico, South Korea, Tanzania and Cuba are considered along with a brief description of the controversial search for a 'third path' in Jamaica between 1972 and 1980.

Finally, some tentative conclusions are advanced which seek to provide a sensible definition of development and an understanding of the political process as it relates to national development. Attempts to over-simplify development as a purely economic phenomenon are examined. Equally, the fallacy of believing that greater capacity can be achieved in spite of the political process, as if there were some means of magically separating the two, is exposed. It is also contended that there can be no real, properly understood and continuing development in the Third World as the result of isolated national effort. The necessity for international action both amongst Third World countries and between the Third World, the developed world, the Soviet Union and East European countries, is advocated as an indispensable part of development itself.

Today many commentators argue about whether a Third World exists. Indeed recently a book has been published entitled *The End of the Third World*, written by economist Nigel Harris.

For the purposes of this book the Third World comprises all those parts of the globe which were conquered and, to a greater or lesser extent, colonised between the sixteenth and twentieth centuries. More particularly, the term applies to countries which, beginning with that common experience, sought and won their political independence. This begins with Latin America in the early nineteenth century and continues to the present time where a number of mini states in the Caribbean have achieved their independence.

When discussing the Third World it is important to

remember the great complexity of the social, political and economic structures that it involves. The range of ideological commitment to be found within the whole group must also be borne in mind. The group will include everything from Saudi Arabia, newly emerging from feudal monarchy, to the semi-military dictatorships still to be found in parts of Latin America. There are viable, independent, traditional democracies like Jamaica and Venezuela; together with democratic one-party states such as Tanzania (paradoxical as that may seem to traditionally attuned Western ears) and undemocratic one-party states like Burma. It even includes strict Marxist/Leninist states like Cuba.

The Western mind is constantly confounded by the fact that 97 of these states, representing the full range of the ideological and social spectrum, should find a common meeting ground in the Movement of Non-Aligned Countries. Equally, the fact that the more than 100 states which make up the Group of 77 in the United Nations, involving an even wider range than is represented in the Non-Aligned Movement, find it possible to make common cause on many issues in the United Nations system, is a source of surprise and even irritation. All this is possible because there is an underlying and binding cement to be found in their common experience of imperialism and colonialism together with the common disadvantages they suffer under the present world economic structure.

As to the notion of development, it is critical to bear in mind that there is no one complete form of political, social and economic organisation which represents the ideal to be sought by all people regardless of their experience and their circumstances. Development is to do with more and better houses, more and better medical services, more and better education, more and better vacations and more secure and happier retirement. It is to do with the economic growth necessary to support these aspirations. It is necessarily to do with economic control. And it is ultimately to do with a happier and more self-fulfilling experience during one's working life which must begin with happier and more constructively engaged children. These elements will be common to all perceptions. But how to accomplish this, in what order and as a consequence of what sacrifice by which group, will be influenced by the particular experience of a particular people. Therefore, development has to be understood as representing the search of one set of people for the fulfilment of the goals which it can set for itself. This in turn implies the capacity of a nation to mobilise its people to exploit their opportunities so that they contribute directly to those goals.

In all of this there is a political process both in the definition of goals and their attainment; there is a social process which both contributes to the attainment of those goals and which is, itself, affected by their attainment; and, of course, there is an economic process without which it is idle to define goals and impossible to accomplish them.

It is important that clear definition be given to words that may cause confusion, such as imperialism.

This word is extraordinarily controversial in modern usage. It has become so much the creature of different people's diverse perspectives within the world political process that some have refused to use it on the grounds that it has become jargonised – lost in the political rhetoric. Furthermore, imperialism is an important process of world history and as such there is much in the contemporary world that will be difficult to understand if it is not adequately defined, as perhaps:

Any form of domination of one people by another which has as its objective and, in fact, ensures the transfer of wealth from the dominated to the dominator. Imperialism does not come to an end when a particular country achieves its political independence. If the economic organisation remains sufficiently in foreign hands it will continue to be subjected to foreign domination and exploitation to the benefit of the external power.

This definition seeks to encompass a broad range of historical experience. Of course for those who prefer the Marxist discipline, there is the classical definition of imperialism as capitalism in its final and highest stage of development.

One also has to bear in mind an older idea which sought to identify and equate imperialism with only the political conquest of one people by another and their control within an empire regardless of what internal relationships might be. For reasons which will emerge, it is felt that this definition is inadequate.

Then, of course, one has to remember the apologists, people like Cecil Rhodes who saw imperialism as a great mission. There were others who had even quainter notions, stating that the whole acquisition of an empire happened quite accidentally and coined the marvellous phrase – 'The British Empire had been acquired in a fit of absence of mind.'

One other concept that has to be distinguished and which will be dealt with later in the series is the concept of hegemony, because there is an important distinction between hegemony and imperialism – a distinction that was discussed in *Jamaica: Struggle in the Periphery*, pp. 216–17.

Another word to be defined is colonialism. This is a similar concept and a definition might read:

Colonialism is the process by which a native people are brought under external political control by settlement following conquest.

This direct political control facilitates economic domination as well. Colonialism is therefore direct political control of one country over another.

Today the world has an extraordinary productive capacity. For example, it is currently producing food that is equivalent to more than 2,400 calories per capita per day, where the scientists tell us that about 2,350 calories a day give us an adequate diet without problems of enlarged waistlines. Yet, that same world which already produces more than enough to feed its entire population is looking at 12 million children dying each year of protein deficiency.

The world possesses an enormous range of scholarship; vast accumulated experience of political processes; of government systems and the science of government; of social justice; it has been able to create this phenomenon of interdependence through instant communication and computerised knowledge. Out of all of that have emerged perceptions of an ethical ideal. And yet, that same world now has a situation where, as the Brandt Commission Report states,

> The North, including Eastern Europe, has a quarter of the world's population and four-fifths of its income; the South, including China, has four billion people – three-quarters of the world's population, but living on one-fifth of the world's income.

This situation is obviously socially dangerous and is an affront ethically. An enquiry must be made as to how this came to be and what can be done about it.

1
Mercantile Capitalism:
The Beginning of the Process

An historical examination must begin at a particular
point when there is the kind of political relationship
between various social groups that permits a spontaneous economic evolution without interference from
each other. A social group far back in antiquity would
approach production in a very simple and logical way.
It would seek to produce what it needs with the means
at hand and apply the skills it possesses. But what is
crucial is that it would produce what it needs with the
same means at hand.

In due course, there may be advances in organisation
and knowledge, or in a technological discovery and it
may start to produce more than it needs. It is then able
to enter into a process of exchange for the first time
and will seek some other group, somewhere, that may
produce in a different framework that has something
to exchange. At this point you can begin to have, logically, an international division of labour that is based
on mutual advantage. But the key to what takes place,
of course, is the production of what is needed, the significance of which will become apparent as the book
proceeds.

Here comparison should be made with what has
actually happened to the world. At the end of the long
colonial experience enormous areas of the globe were
geared to produce, not what was needed for themselves

or for exchange for mutual advantage, but rather had been compelled to be the producers of what others needed. In turn they found it necessary to import what they needed.

So for the first time in history a complete reversal of all economic logic occurred. Huge areas of the earth's surface could not produce and export in response to their own needs. Rather they became totally dependent on the dictates of an external source. Worse than that was the fact that those sections of the productive process that were available to them were those having the least sophistication, and the least capacity to develop what is called 'value added'. It is not surprising that such a process created a world in which there is a vast concentration of the means of production, technology and capital in a relatively small part of the world.

To illustrate this thought one might recall the experience of a certain product in a country like Jamaica, which was developed for centuries as one extended sugar plantation. Jamaica grew sugar cane and was allowed to grind the cane into wet sugar in Jamaican mills because it would have been too expensive to ship the bulky cane across the Atlantic to Britain. That sugar would then enter into an economic process involving technology, shipping and capital. The process would result in the making of a profit. It would then cross the Atlantic to London and enter a port where another sophisticated economic process would begin. It was then put on the railway line to arrive at a refinery where the white crystallised sugar would be produced.

The cocoa bean grown in Ghana, West Africa (the Gold Coast as it was then called) has a similar tale. It goes through exactly the same process, the same 'value added' occurring across the Atlantic as it is transported to a cocoa refinery in England. Marry the sugar and the cocoa and a chocolate bar is produced. That chocolate bar, of course, is then an important adjunct to English taste and enjoyment. But the story is not yet finished. The confectionery then crosses railways, the Atlantic, and ports to the original people who grew the sugar cane and grew the cocoa bean who now buy that same chocolate bar with all the 'value added' and profits made both ways across the Atlantic. There is a sense in which this story is oversimplified, but it reveals the heart of the economic process that shaped the Third World within which so many of us are trapped.

Now, the historical question is asked, 'How did all this happen?'

Many historians have concluded that the world of the fifteenth century did not reflect great disparities in the capacity of a number of more advanced societies in comparison with Europe.

By that century China dominated ocean trade with Africa. So advanced was China's civilisation that as late as 1793, the Emperor of China informed King George III, 'As your Ambassador can see for himself we possess all things. I set no value on objects strange or ingenious and have no use for your country's manufactures.'

In Africa by that same century there had been the rise and decline of many great empires. These included the empire in Ghana in the tenth century, the Mali empire of the eleventh to thirteenth century, famous for the city of Timbuktu. The historian, Basil Davidson, describes African societies at that time in this way: 'More often though, there would be peasants whose status differed little in essence from that of the serfs of medieval Europe who were also regarded as inseparable from the land they tilled.'

In India the bulk of the population lived in village communities, each of which was a functionally integrated agricultural and handicraft economy, based on the communal ownership of land, on well defined individual production and social responsibilities. The nature of Indian society led Karl Marx to develop the notion of the 'Asiatic mode of production' as distinct from European feudalism. Whether or not this mode would have led to capitalist development is speculative since by the nineteenth century India was firmly incorporated into the world capitalist system.

In the Americas there were a variety of civilisations at different stages of development. They ranged from Arawaks in Jamaica who were in a state akin to that of primitive communalism to highly civilised states in South America. Gunder Frank explains,

> In South America from their seat in the Andean Cuzco and their ritual capital Machu Picchu, the Incas had only recently conquered and subdued an area stretching several thousand miles from the equator well into present-day Chile and Bolivia ... in several aspects the Inca society was more highly developed than even that of the Aztecs including agricultural terracing and irrigation, mining and fishing, transportation (using the llama as a pack animal) and communication by courier, which they used to extend their conquest, dominion and division of labour.

What about Europe? By the eleventh century feudalism had consolidated its hold and in the twelfth and thirteenth centuries commercial activities began to develop rapidly. In the early fifteenth century Europe had recovered from the plagues of the Middle Ages. There was also the development of agricultural technology and the production of manufactures. All these elements combined to push Europe to develop new trade routes and to find new sources of precious metals. Again Gunder Frank gives a vivid description.

Throughout the fifteenth century, the Italian city-states, especially Venice, Florence, Milan and Genoa, had served as intermediaries in the spice trade between the Moslems in the East and the Norther-Europeans in the West. Furthermore, they had developed their own manufacturing and had established sugar plantations based on local and imported slave labour in Palestine and Mediterranean islands such as Cyprus and Crete.

(It is therefore not strange that Christopher Columbus was an Italian.)

With the exception of the Americas which were not 'discovered' until the late fifteenth century the world was pulled together by a network of trading relationships. At the same time the similar level of technological and economic development of the trading partners means that trade was carried out to the mutual advantage of both.

Trade was then the critical element and therefore traders became a special social group. With the development of trade came monopoly privileges and regulations concerning products. By the fifteenth century power had passed from the craftsmen to the traders. The hegemony of merchant capital was being established. With the 'discovery' of the Americas, merchants came to dominate the world of the fifteenth to the eighteenth century. The direction of the trade currents shifted. Venice and South German cities no longer had a geographical advantage. Now the countries along the Atlantic seaboard had the edge. Frank states: 'The discoveries opened up a period of magnificent expansion in the entire economic life of Western Europe.'

The extension of the market has always been one of the strongest spurs to economic activity. At this point this extension of the market was greater than anything that had ever happened before. New places with which to trade, new markets for the goods of your own country, new goods to bring back home – it was all very infectious and stimulating and ushered in a period of intense commercial activity and of further discovery, exploration and expansion.

All this gave impetus to European shipbuilding skills – skills which had been learned from the Arabs in the days of the Greek city-states and the Vikings. The skills in navigation, geography and cartography provided a critical edge that in many ways started the enormous historical process that is unfolding even to this time. People like Vasco Da Gama sailed around the Cape of Good Hope and opened up trade to the Far East. Columbus pursued his more familiar exploits; and then Cabot began the exploration of North America in 1496. So, beginning with this great period of the explorers, the five phases recognised as being part of the whole process of the birth and development of imperialism commence.

In the first phase (from about 1500 to 1650) there was the rise of commercial capital in Europe and the development of world commerce in a systematic way. The critical means that was available at this time was naval power. In that period certain clear objectives were being pursued by very clear means. These were first, the attempt by the Europeans to dominate trade; and in this they succeeded. The Europeans also defeated the Arabs and Asians who had controlled trade up to that time. There was the search for spices because that was an important part of curing meat for winter storage; and for gold and silver, particularly by the Spanish, to be used as a means of exchange. In the course of all of this the rudiments of the colonial system were being established although the objectives were really quite simple at the time. Indeed in retrospect there was nothing really complicated or even particularly ambitious about it.

Mostly, the colonialism of that time, because power was primarily naval in scope, was an island colonialism concentrating for instance on the Caribbean islands and on the establishment of trading posts in the coastal areas of Africa and India, which was about as far as it went during this period.

At that very time, the European states were beginning to lay the foundations for modern and sophisticated economic development by standardising items such as coinage, weights and measures, and by providing security systems within which people could effectively develop commercial structures. These two developments, going hand in hand, led to the second phase, moving the world from a rudimentary stage to a period when the structures which were to entrench the colonial system – which so fundamentally shaped the world and all that has happened since – began to be established. It is in this second phase (again with naval power at the heart of the capacity to make it work) that the establishment of what became known as the mercantile system is found. This system established a geographical division of labour, including the exchange of English manufactures for tropical and semi-tropical products organised by English merchants and carried abroad on English ships. For the system to work trade was critical.

The mercantile system became consolidated when in 1660 Britain passed what were known as the Navigation Acts. The Acts represent a turning point in history and read:

> ... for the increase of shipping and encouragement of the navigation of this nation ... be it enacted ... that from and after the first day of December One Thousand Six Hundred and Sixty ... no goods or commodities whatsoever shall be imported into or exported out of any lands, island plantations or territories belonging to His Majesty or in his possession in Asia, Africa or America, in any other ship or vessel as do truly and without fraud belong only to the people of England or Ireland or Dominion of Wales or ... built and belonging to any of the said lands, islands, plantations or territories, as the right owners thereof and whereof the master and three–fourths of the mariners at least are English ...

At one stroke the Navigation Acts crystallised the essence of the nature of the period of mercantile colonisation which was the British control of trade and the direction of trade and production. Associated with that process was another very important evolutionary step – the slave trade.

What was the basis of the slave trade? Having wiped out most of the Indian populations in the Caribbean and parts of coastal America, and being determined to produce cotton for British industry and sugar for British and European tables, the colonial powers had to search for a source of cheap labour. What more logical than to apply slave labour to these extensive plantations of cotton and sugar.

But there was a further feature to this which is brilliantly analysed by Eric Williams in *Capitalism and*

Slavery and which was termed the triangular trade. The triangular trade became a third important evolutionary feature of the process. In essence, ships would leave British ports with British exports. These exports, destined for West Africa where they were exchanged for slaves, became an important additional outlet for British manufacturing. Of course, very substantial profits would be made on that first part of the journey. Slaves would then be transferred to the Caribbean and to the United States where they would be bought and again a very substantial accumulation of profit on the second leg of the triangle was realised. Then, on the third leg the sugar, cotton, or whatever it might be, would come back to Britain to complete the triangle with very hefty gains, naturally and logically made at all three stages.

That the slave trade was a social and moral outrage is a separate matter. Fundamentally the triangular trade was a tremendous source of expansion for British industry and, of course, a tremendous accumulator of capital. Eric Williams argues that a lot of the subsequent capital accumulation which financed the industrial revolution was amassed out of the triangular trade.

As phase two developed, with the restructuring of trade relationships and concentration of wealth taking place, the seeds of the third phase were being sown. This ushered in the industrial revolution. This revolution started with the invention of the 'Spinning Jenny' and the steam engine in the eighteenth century and set in train a number of new developments that are important.

This industrial revolution created the need for more markets and because of increased wealth, there was a far greater capacity to finance military activity. European colonialism moved off the coastline and into the hinterland. Africa was now challenged not only by a series of trading posts along the coast, but was increasingly being explored, exploration bringing conquest in its wake.

In this regard it is important to note that between 1800 and 1870 the area of the earth's surface that was brought within the colonial empire had increased from 35 per cent to a remarkable 67 per cent. So, entering the 1870s, which is just over one hundred years ago, the situation is that well over half of the world is part of the system of structured colonial control. This structure supplies raw materials for the needs of the centre and ensures a much larger market for the burgeoning industrial capacity of Britain and Europe.

The fourth and fifth stages can be covered rapidly as they occurred more quickly. In the 1870s there was the first great depression of the capitalist system in what is called the First World. A *British Royal Commission in the 1870s* investigated the problem and came to the following conclusion:

> We think that overproduction has been one of the most prominent features of the course of trade during recent years; and that the depression under which we are now suffering may be particularly explained by this fact. The remarkable feature of the present situation, and that which in our opinion distinguishes it from all previous periods of depression is the length of time during which overproduction has continued. We are satisfied that in recent years, and more particularly in the years during which the depression of Trade has prevailed, the production of commodities generally and the accumulation of capital in this country have been proceeding at a rate more rapid than the increase of population.

It is significant that this period ushered in an important feature in the development of imperialism, that of the increasing tendency to monopoly. As businesses crashed in the depression there was a rush of mergers with larger firms consuming weaker ones. The result was the concentration in economic ownership and control.

Also associated with this, as part of the evolving sophistication of the system, was the first emergence of finance capital with banks playing an increasingly significant role in the economic process.

At the same time what is sometimes called the second industrial revolution was moving the productive world from the steam engine to the combustion engine, developing electricity and searching for oil as a source of energy. This, of course, led to an even greater need for controlled markets and a deeper entrenchment of the system. By the 1870s, it is fair to say that a complete system of world trade and finance was in place. You can actually trace the processes by which the spread of the colonial structure and the increasing sophistication of economic organisation finally put a total system in place.

By 1914 the area of the earth's surface controlled or dominated by the centres of the imperial system – Britain, France, Germany, Portugal, Holland – had grown to 84.5 per cent. By the time of the First World War eight-tenths of humankind lived in a colonial state.

By the end of that war the fifth phase that completed both the structure and the picture was ready: the age of the multinational corporation. The period between 1918 and 1945 was dominated by the emergence of these organisations.

What exactly is meant by a multinational corporation? This system has the following key elements:

ownership of the means of production, control of trade mechanisms, control of the manufacturing process and of the marketing and service mechanisms. Multinational corporations are able to marry all these inputs in the production of a particular commodity, rendering geographical zones redundant.

Adding the multinational system to all that went before completes what some call the imperialist process. No matter what it is called, it is a world economic structure which has certain characteristics which include domination. The nature of this structure is the source of many problems of our times.

By 1945, when the great national liberation struggles began, what was in place was a structure of economic control whose roots went as far back as the seventeenth century, to the mercantile system. The features of that model anticipated many of the elements of the present problem. First, there was the question of what some scholars called the centre–periphery relationship, meaning that one whole area of the earth has grown up as an appendage to the economic needs of another area. Secondly, the elimination of indigenous colonial production created the phenomenon of *structural dependence*. Once this was in place, the industrial revolution led to a series of colonial developments which completed the internationalisation of this model.

Finally, in the post-industrialised period all the various elements have combined to create a particular set of relationships in the world economy. Increasingly, the economic process grew out of reach of the political process. Capitalism was born out of the nation state. However, the creation of world markets and the logic of competition with the resultant tendency for concentration meant that corporations soon outgrew national boundaries. As this happened, national political processes became objectively irrelevant. How, for example, does a national political process affect the production of a Ford Escort when its various parts are made in different countries? Hence, the heart of the problem of the multinational corporation has nothing to do with its productive capacity. It is, in fact, a very efficient means of production and distribution rationalised under one system of ownership. However, it has become removed from accountability; removed from responsiveness to the nation state's political process and therefore harder to control.

In the face of all these things national liberation struggles were inevitable and the next chapter will analyse the nature of these struggles. More importantly, however, an attempt will be made to set a framework within which an understanding of the experience of 80 per cent of the world can be pursued. The economic structures will be examined that existed in the mid-1940s, when the great liberation drives began which eventually led to the flags of freedom waving so bravely in the winds of change and in the face of adversity. What were the political and cultural realities of the time? What was bequeathed to humanity by the long history of modern imperialism? When attention is drawn to that legacy the shaping of the liberation processes can be seen as well as how they, in turn, shaped attempts at development. Consideration will be given as to why there has been a continuing and massive failure in the development of most of the Third World, which will hopefully reveal the answer to the question, 'What can be done about it all?'

2
The Consolidation of the System

This study so far has attempted to isolate common factors in the world's complex diversity of historical processes and then to examine the interaction of the Third World with these processes. This approach is important because out of commonality may emerge an outline of possible strategies. An examination of the condition of the world will demonstrate how critical it is for us to evolve a strategy for Third World development.

One must remember what the economic process is about and for clarity's sake the obvious must be restated. There are four very clear phases of the economic process. One is the phase which deals primarily and simply with input. In a sense the input is either the crop that is cultivated, the animal that is reared or the mineral extracted from the ground. From there the product goes through increasingly complex processes which prepare it for the satisfaction of need. This second phase involves everything that modern economic development is about. The conversion may involve complex chemical processes, it may involve refining, combining items, altering chemical structures, constructing, or fabricating.

That conversion process promotes the critical developments of technology and ancillary forms of human activity, and broadens the structure, complexity and reach of economies. Out of all that complexity emerges the capacity to produce more, the capacity therefore to generate greater means of satisfying human needs and greater wealth.

The third phase is that of moving the product to satisfy human need and consumption. Therefore the whole economies of transport and shipping are involved in the process.

However, consumption is no longer limited to food, clothing and shelter, but is subject to another and fourth economic process which stimulates the need to acquire unnecessary things. Stimulated appetites soon transfer into the category of need. All these things are very important and are mentioned now, not to labour the obvious, but because in the later complexities of the challenge of development, every single one of these things at some stage becomes a critical problem in the management of an economy.

Very often when one reads in the newspapers of a particular Third World country with a foreign exchange crisis there is a reflex tendency to think ... 'That's because Third World countries cannot manage their economies.' Yet when inside the problem, inside the decision-making process, from the perspective of the political directorate, one begins to see two critical factors. On the one hand the ability to bring resources to bear within the economy as the means of satisfying people's needs is fundamentally conditioned by the structure that has been inherited. On the other hand there are severe limits to the capacity of that structure to produce and to provide foreign exchange and, hence, to satisfy needs.

The newly independent country begins with a deformed economy that makes disproportionate demands on foreign exchange because it has been structured in a manner that drains what little margin

of foreign exchange is available. It is necessary, therefore, to work back and enquire why. How did the trap
happen? It is then discovered that efforts made to
move out of the state of underdevelopment and to
provide a more complex structure involve deeper problems within the world economy.

For example, the Jamaican economy first began to
feel the crunch of the foreign exchange crisis in 1974.
Members of the political directorate sat down for the
first time and looked at the question: how does this
economy that was for 320 years a part of the colonial
experience work? At that time the economy was
heavily dependent on the primary products of sugar
and bauxite, with a supplement from tourism. A manufacturing sector had also begun to develop. However
it became clear that this manufacturing crust, not
resting upon a raw material base or native technology,
continued to trap the country inside the world structures in a dependent position. Relying upon the
importation of a number of raw materials, spare parts,
technology, machinery, etc. it was a net drain upon
foreign exchange rather than a net earner of this indispensable component of growth. But there could be no
question of dismantling this sector because of the
social consequences, including unemployment. All
those little factories that made shirts and other articles
represented employment in an economy that is still
unable to put 20 per cent of its people to work. The
political dilemma is obvious.

If it is argued, theoretically, that a particular enterprise is a net loser of foreign exchange and therefore a
burden, that it is not really contributing, then the
nation must know how it will deal with the thousands
of factory workers and their families who, for the time
being, are involved in that particular activity. The

problems of foreign exchange cannot solely determine policy without creating a crisis. Yet the fear of such a crisis may leave the political directorate less able to pursue strategic remedies.

Economic Structures

To understand the present state of the world capitalist system a certain historical evolution must be kept in mind. This begins, of course, with the mercantile system. What the mercantile system did between the first adventure of Columbus and the coming of the industrial revolution was to establish the fundamental contours of a world economy just beginning to be born. It established the system in which, by contrivance, areas of the earth became the producers of the basic inputs of the world economic process. These areas were attached to a centre that would be the processor. The colony became the periphery that grew the raw material and the imperial centre became the authority commanding and controlling output for the productive process from growth to consumption. It is at this point that the colony rejoins the economic process as a rather impoverished part of the market.

All this is rudimentary and originally the mercantile system was dominated by the movement of spices and precious metals. It had not become a fully articulated process at that stage.

What the industrial revolution accomplished, apart from revolutionising the capacity to produce at the centre, was to make the supply of raw materials even more important. It also became imperative to command and expand the market, because there was now a capacity to produce more than could be consumed within a particular society. So, with the mercantile system having established the movement of the inputs from the periphery, the industrial revolution escalated production, created more power, and in structural terms made the reverse movement back to the market imperative. The colony now became important both as the source of raw materials and as a market for surplus production.

This puts in place the two elements that are fundamental to modern structures: access to raw materials and markets. Then came the age of monopoly ownership which has many elements that are significant. One of these had special significance. The growth of monopoly had started during the nineteenth century and came to its height after the slump of the 1870s. Its importance lay in its association with the main source of finance in the productive process. This had two implications.

First, as monopoly ownership increased it began to set the stage for what later became a system of international control and management of the world economic process. As long as there was a situation in Britain (and other similar countries) where a great number of firms, in keeping with the old theories of Adam Smith, were producing within the capitalist system, their sheer numbers made it impossible to meet and plan what was to happen. When monopoly began to emerge in answer to some of the contradictions of the earlier stage, it set in train a new dimension. Then as finance capital increasingly replaced the personal capitalist of the nineteenth century, there was a change in the organisation of production, creating a kind of professional, co-operative, monopolistic management. This set the stage for increasingly centralised control of the operation of the economy.

Two critical elements, technology and power, have to be remembered when moving from the mercantile system to the industrial revolution and to the age of monopoly because they are fundamental historically and have a relevance today. The mercantile system could start because there was naval power; the conquest could take place because there was gunpowder; slavery was a vital means in the development of the plantation system that was so important; the industrial revolution is critical in terms of the mechanical inventions it produced and the development of steam. And the age of steam is important because it has a bearing on power. It has a bearing on naval power, it makes possible the railway and the conquest of the interior, where a coastal phenomenon becomes continentalised; power and technology always work hand in hand.

By 1914 the world had reached a very interesting stage. It had produced a single capitalist economy with all the outlines carefully articulated as to where the raw materials came from, how the process of market development took place, the control of the process. All the elements were in place. World capitalism was now established as an integrated productive structure. All that was missing was a political understanding of what all this implied.

A bizarre period follows between 1914 and 1945 when the system was established but those who had the decision-making powers did not understand its workings. The cartel managers knew that the system was in place, but the politicians did not and so there was uncertainty as to how to manage this new phenomenon.

In the meantime, following the Treaty of Berlin in 1884, the European powers finally carved out the empires and carved up Africa. A result of the intense rivalry was the First World War.

Incredibly stupid things were done under the system after the war. Germany was punished and reparations exacted. At another level, even more irrationally, things occurred because people had not learned how to manage the new productive capacity and handle its internal contradictions. So, between 1919 and 1939 three countries became historical aberrations. One was Germany which became expansionist and prepared for yet another war. Italy began to move into Africa as it tried to use political and military power to claw a special place for itself. And Japan started to move into China. All of this made war more likely. There were examples of countries which, when faced with a problem of foreign exchange and feeling in danger of losing out in trade, began retaliatory trade wars. The major nations started to fight each other with currency depreciations and devaluations as each tried to establish a special advantage. This period was interesting because those who created and managed the world structure did not fully understand what existed and were lashing about in irrational and irrelevant ways.

What awaited resolution was the contradiction between the international economy and the nation state. The world now had an economy which was increasingly an integrated international phenomenon. Meanwhile, the nation state played host to the separate parts of this world system of production and distribution. But this was still a nation state reflecting outmoded strategies of competitive aggressiveness. The attempt to create an international system of political management of the world economy was to await *Bretton Woods** and the post Second World War world. The old nation states were then beginning to learn that they did not need to fight each other but could do

* See Appendix for an explanation of this Agreement.

better by co-operating to preserve their collective control and power.

By 1945 it became clear that the system required international management. There was the recognition of the need to prepare an overall international policy, an international set of arrangements that would express the logic of the reality and enshrine the structures that were to be built.

It is suggested that the critical factor that made the *Bretton Woods* discussions possible at the end of the Second World War and created a new set of structures was the emergence of the power of the United States. What is important about the United States is, first of all, that it was not itself involved in the traditional nation state hostilities of Europe. As a relatively new political economic creation, it was not imprisoned in old attitudes and brought a sort of cool, calculating, pragmatic detachment to this world economy – what should be done about it, how to protect and perpetuate it?

The second important consideration was that the United States had tremendous investments and growing involvement in Latin America and Africa and was by then the beneficiary of enormous returns on these investments.

When this was added to a world in which Germany had been completely flattened, and Britain virtually impoverished, the stage was set to have as the dominant actor on the world's stage one quite untrammelled by the quarrels of ancient and irrelevant nation states anxious to create an integrated world economy; very anxious that nonsensical notions like nations protecting their economies against the intrusion of other people's production should be abolished; anxious that its own productive machinery should have access to the cheapest possible materials; anxious that its enormous capacity should be able to have access to markets even apart from its own enormous internal market; anxious to create a world in which there could be a return to a modified form of free trade, not in the classic sense of Adam Smith, but an economy in which raw materials could be bought in accordance with natural advantage and sold without let or hindrance.

It is clear that the United States was able to prevail upon the rest of the capitalist world to go along with the new game plan because, to begin with, it had a power that was irresistible. Other actors in the world capitalist situation had begun to recognise that a new kind of organisation of production was possible involving United States capital and to a lesser degree the capital of Britain, Germany and France. In fact, this was the dawn of the dominance of the multinational corporation and what has been termed, 'multilateral capitalism'.

It was the institutions which were created which made things work. The United Nations system was set up to keep peace. West Germany, of course, was treated with instant and comprehensive generosity because it was very important to get that country fully back on its feet as a progressive and full participant in a world capitalist system. To be able to finance all of this, the International Bank of Reconstruction and Development,* now called the World Bank, was created. Its purpose was explicitly to pave the way for the spread of foreign investment and private foreign capital throughout the world.

The World Bank was set up originally to be a precursor to movements of private foreign capital, either by the provision of infrastructure or sometimes as an underwriter of that kind of development. To try to

* See Appendix for explanation.

make sure that there was no retreat into a world of destructive trade wars, the General Agreement on Tariffs and Trade (GATT)* was established. This was to work quietly and systematically through the decades, to open up trade. Finally, and very importantly on the economic side, the International Monetary Fund (IMF)* was set up to stop any possibility that particular nations might upset the applecart by handling their foreign exchange problems unilaterally and without reference to the general preservation of the orderly and balanced operation of the system. Of course, all of that had to have its own instrument of power and that was provided by the North Atlantic Treaty Organisation (NATO).

When stripping all the details to their essence, the significance of this period is that at long last the world capitalist system had evolved in terms of its own logic to the point where economic nationalism, a very important element in building the process at one stage, was now contained. It was put in its proper perspective where it could not introduce irrelevant, extraneous and aberrant behaviour to disturb growth and consolidation. It is a matter of record that from 1945 to the present there has been a phenomenal explosion of productive capacity within the control of the multinational corporation (the transnational corporation as it is sometimes called). The distinguishing element of this explosion is that it separates the economic process from any form of national political accountability, putting it virtually beyond the reach of any national political process. Furthermore, the corporation is able to more completely express the implications of the model that started with the mercantile system. This model is the idea that one factor of production is

* See Appendix for an explanation.

created in one place by planning; is then married to a conversion process somewhere else; is then moved all over the world in a planned operation by a central, multilateral, multinational arrangement to end up finally in consumption at various points of the globe.

Thus was created, on the one hand, the rational optimisation of productive capacity internationally. However, from another point of view a Frankenstein was created for those who were marginalised by the process.

Seven elements emerged from the examination of this process. First, production in the colonial empire was substantially confined to phase one of the economic process either by the natural growth of the system as it was ordained or by the destruction of anything that got in its path.

Secondly, by 1945, much of the means of production that existed in the colonial world was owned in the centres of power by the foreign capital exported from those centres.

Thirdly, these areas of carefully contrived exploitation were taxed out of their extraordinarily limited means to finance the very apparatus of oppression that kept them in place. It is absolutely amazing to see how little the colonial empire cost the centres of empire.

Fourthly, there is the brutal compression of wages so as to ensure the maximisation of profit, even when moving away from slavery which was the extreme form.

Fifthly, primary products were organised in unequal exchange with goods that the colonies were forced to import.

Sixthly, even the third economic phase – the moving of goods – was manipulated. Not only was it appropriated to the centres of power, but was used as a further means of manipulating the relationship and the exchange between the two parts.

And finally, there is the question of how the centres of power were able to appropriate surpluses created by the trade that was directed from the big economies themselves.

When discussing confinement to the first phase of primary production, it is interesting to note that in 1939 sugar, which was the dominant factor of Caribbean colonialism, represented 80 per cent of the exports of Cuba; 50 per cent of the exports of Puerto Rico; 67 per cent of the exports of the Dominican Republic and in certain small islands of the English speaking Caribbean, it was up to 90 per cent of the total exports. In Africa production was compressed into nuts, palm oil, jute, copper, tea and minerals. Very importantly, apart from the obvious consequences of this phenomenon, there was the history of the deliberate destruction of such industry as existed at the time of the coming of imperialism and the establishment of the colonies.

History records that the entire handicraft industry which was indigenous to Africa, Asia, India, a handicraft industry that in itself was reflective of at least a self-contained economic process, was quickly wiped out by the competitive advantage of the products of the industrial revolution. In this regard the case of India is instructive.

At the time when Wellington finally consolidated British power in India, India had quite a vibrant textile industry that used to export vigorously to Britain. There are figures that demonstrate the process of destruction of indigenous capacity. In 1814, the value of finished textile cotton goods from India to the United Kingdom market was £1.3 million a year. By 1835 the Indian textile exports to England were virtually wiped out to a paltry £100,000.

The conversion process forced India to become wrenched and deformed into a commodity supplier. In the same year, 1814, India exported 9 million pounds in weight of raw cotton to Britain. By 1933, when the exports of the finished goods had collapsed, she was sending 32 million pounds, and by 1944, 88 million pounds of raw cotton. And so the experience unfolds, with the colonial empire becoming one great plantation and/or mine.

In terms of the ownership of the means of production, there are very useful analyses of this in the writings of Galeano, Eric Williams and Walter Rodney. There is a clear analysis of the US penetration of the Caribbean, and ownership of Caribbean sugar during the 1920s and 1930s, in Williams' *From Columbus to Castro*. In this process there are interesting sidelights as to how the colonial state and its apparatus of power facilitated the ownership of the means of production. Two examples from thousands are chosen because they are so dramatic.

Once Kenya was brought to heel by imperialism, there was a Lord Delamere who actually bought 100,000 acres at one penny per acre.

In Liberia in 1926, the Firestone Rubber Company was able, under the umbrella of US power, to buy one million acres of land at 6 cents per acre. All that was required was to give to the government of Liberia 1 per cent of the value of the rubber that it extracted.

In fact, there was the famous Colonel Grogan, who when Kenya had finally been subdued and the Kikuyu finally alienated from their land, made this interesting remark: 'We have stolen the land of the Kikuyu, we must now steal his limbs because to get his labour is a logical corollary of the process.' That is when men like Cecil Rhodes, for example, found an ingenious way of compelling people to labour in the Transvaal. A tax of 10 shillings was extracted unless a peasant farmer could prove that he had worked three months for some white farmer or in some mining activity. Being unable to pay this tax, working for 9 pence a day, he had to sell his land in the end. And so he was slowly wrenched off the land into the mines; if he went below to mine he got a shilling a day.

The question of the third factor is that there is very little evidence that any part of the empire ever cost any of the centres of power anything. Concerning the compression of wages, a very compelling illustration is found in Walter Rodney's *How Europe Underdeveloped Africa*, where he prepared an analysis of the labour costs involved in shipping goods from West Africa to the US. Apples were carefully compared with apples and oranges with oranges. This involved the same amount of exports one way and exports the other way and the total wages paid for the complete process both ways. As late as 1955 the same amount of goods moving over the US docks drew five-sixths of the wage bill while the same goods moving across the West African docks drew one-sixth.

Then there is the factor of unequal exchange. It has been calculated that in the period between 1870 and 1930 African exports were only able to purchase some 60 per cent of what they could purchase in the earlier period – there had been a catastrophic fall of some 40 per cent in the terms of trade. Jamaica's experience comes to mind. When Jamaica became independent in 1962, a tractor could be financed with the proceeds of 18 tons of sugar; by 1980 it took 60 tons of sugar to finance the same tractor. This equation was a clear indication of unequal exchange and abounds throughout the colonial experience.

It is also important to look within the process of the exchange to see how skilfully trade was managed. The development of the United Africa Company is well documented. As the years passed in the African experience it acquired a tremendous, almost monopolistic, control over all the ground nuts and palm oil and indeed everything that was produced by the African peasant. At a time when the depression was assaulting the world economy, during 1929, the African farmers' price for palm oil fell from 14 shillings to one shilling and two pence per gallon. The farmers were told that this was an effect of world depression. But it is an interesting fact that at the same time the United Africa Company continued to make tremendous profits and maintained its 15 per cent dividend on ordinary shares throughout the entire period.

A final example of this manipulation of the unequal exchange: as part of the contribution to the Second World War effort, countries like the then Gold Coast had to suffer a fall in the price of cocoa from £50 per ton to £10. This is ironic because at the very time when they were making this great sacrifice, the price they were paying for khaki had moved from 3 shillings to 10 shillings a yard and the price for iron sheets had moved from 30 shillings to 100 shillings each. So the war apparently was having no negative effect on the trade the other way.

When looking at shipping it is the same story. In *How Europe Underdeveloped Africa* Rodney points out that African produce, despite increased volumes, could not attract a reduced shipping charge. The rates seemed to remain the same. It has been established that during that period, flour being shipped to West Africa drew a freight rate of 35 shillings a ton. The same flour to the United States was shipped at 7 shillings and 6 pence.

Let us look finally at the category of the appropriation of surplus. During the Second World War, Germany overran Belgium. However, for the entire war Belgium ran a government in exile from the surplus of a business in the Congo without having to liquidate one single foreign asset or sell one ounce of gold. There is a dramatic quality to this illustration.

Again, the case of India is particularly illustrative of the way the appropriation of surpluses has evolved over the years. The contribution of the triangular trade of goods to West Africa, slaves to the Caribbean and the southern states and so back to Britain, created much of the accumulated capital that made the industrial revolution possible. In this century, the manipulation of trade surpluses became the substitute mechanism that took the place of the triangular trade in bygone centuries. That arose from the fact that within the empires the earnings of the imperial group created currency for the centre of power which would then issue currency for the particular colonial areas.

This process was perhaps inevitable given the organisation of exports and the extreme poverty within the colonies that the system induced. This has been very interestingly described by Gunder Frank in his book, *Dependent Accumulation and Underdevelopment* looking at the question of capital for the metropole through trade. He states,

This means that in fact even measured at world market prices, even more so if estimated in terms of real value, the underdeveloped part of the world through its excess of merchandise exports over merchandise imports really finances all the rest of the world both directly and indirectly.

Specifically, export surplus of the underdeveloped

countries firstly supplied much of the excess merchandise consumption of Europe represented by the
latter's merchandise export deficit or import surplus.

Secondly, it helped to finance the export surplus of
the United States and British Dominions such as
Canada and Australia to Europe.

Thirdly, it helped domestic investment and development in Europe; and fourthly, helped Europe
finance its foreign investments in the United States
and the Dominions whose development was thereby
accelerated. The underdeveloped countries even
financed much of the foreign investment in
themselves.

Another writer, S.B. Saul, summed up the system in
this way: 'The key to Britain's whole payments pattern
up to the period we are about to discuss, lay in India
financing as she probably did more than two-fifths of
Britain's total deficits.'

These are the seven factors in which the participation of the colonial empire in the system which had
become articulated by 1945 was effectively brought
under its international management. It is deformed; it
is impoverished and it is deprived of means. Hence,
Gunder Frank's entirely relevant phrase that 'the
whole process involved the development of underdevelopment.'

The economic process described above obviously
triggers political responses from those nations marginalised by the historical process. This response will be
analysed in the following chapters.

3
Decolonisation:
The Liberation Struggle

In viewing the decolonisation process, a fundamental distinction must be established at the outset. All social formations involve internal arrangements of power. These power relationships are determined by the nature of the productive process and the classes that form around them. The distinction to be drawn to ensure clarity is between a process of reform and a process of fundamental change sometimes called transformation.

Reform processes are those that accept a given set of power relationships. However, in looking at some of the obvious inequities, injustices, and some of the pain that may be associated with a particular set of power relationships in a society and, in response to an urge towards more reasonable arrangements between people, reform will seek to make certain ameliorative changes. These changes do not alter the fundamental power relationships within a particular system. Hence, for example, a minimum wage law dynamically operated in a given society may enormously ameliorate the suffering of the poor but will not change the relations of power. The same is true of vacation leave or laws that will give women equal pay for equal work; all these reform a system without altering the internal power relationships.

Fundamental change or transformation – for the purpose of discussion – is a process which seeks to

43

alter the power relationships within a society as between classes, groups or individuals. Mainly this must be achieved by altering the manner in which different elements in the society relate to the productive process. For example, to the extent that nationalisation removes ownership of the means of production from the control of the traditional class, to that extent it will qualify the nature of the power relationship. But more importantly, if you democratise the workplace and develop within it genuine access to power on the part of workers, access to decision-making, access to the means by which the surplus is distributed, you will tend to change the power relationships within the industry affected. So it is in that sense that distinctions are drawn between reform which ameliorates and fundamental change which transforms the power relationship. There is a fallacy which must be dismissed. It is sometimes contended that fundamental change is only possible through violent revolution. Violence and armed struggle may very often have to be the midwife of transformation; it may sometimes be impossible without it, as is the case of South Africa. But it is possible to transform power relationships within a society without using violence. Therefore, this popular notion which sees revolution and violence as if they are interchangeable categories in history involves a falsification of the historical and, indeed, the revolutionary process. In essence the revolutionary process is about fundamental change in a society's power relationships. Historically, this means the transfer of political, social and economic power from one class to another. In such situations, the absence or presence of violence and its degree is linked to how staunchly the ruling class defends its status quo. It is therefore more accurate to conceive of revolution and fundamental change as equivalent concepts.

Inevitably when speaking of decolonisation one is speaking of transformation. Decolonisation must deal with, first of all, political power – as between one people dominated by another; with economic power, as between one people and another; with cultural influence and domination; and may even have to deal with ideological domination. All of these things are necessary parts of a decolonisation process if it is to be complete and ultimately transformative. Since decolonisation must alter the fundamental power relationships within a society, it is essentially a revolutionary process although not necessarily a violent one. On the other hand the process is often incomplete – in that it may deal with only certain aspects of the power relationships.

National liberation movements are recognised in modern history as the broad category through which the decolonisation process is pursued. To understand this process and understand the different kinds of national liberation movements through which decolonisation expresses itself, one must set these movements within the context of the history of revolution itself.

The national liberation movement as it is known in today's world is an enormously complex phenomenon because it occurs at a time in history when the struggle for liberation on the part of a particular people is no longer simple in its configuration, simple in its objectives, or simple in its expression. Looked at from an historical perspective, perhaps the phrase 'the good old days' should be used to describe that time in history when it was easier to understand the causes of events. Of course it may only look easier because it is further away. However, when examining the early liberation struggles one is dealing either with a straight case of one group striving to emerge as a nation and needing to throw off the domination of another; or with one class seeking to replace another class in the domination of the productive process and therefore of a particular society; or even sometimes, with one class in a newly formed nation trying to throw off the domination of another class within another nation where the latter is frustrating the emergence of the former.

By the end of the colonial epoch in 1945 modern imperialism had affected so many societies of such vast difference and created a world economy of such complexity that current national liberation movements must inevitably reflect that complexity. This is so for several reasons. First, one must examine the nature of the local social formation and its internal dynamics when the conquest occurs. These are not necessarily foreclosed by the external pressure. Secondly, one must remember the impact of colonial economic development on the subject peoples. It will create new beneficiaries and victims in greater or lesser degrees. Thirdly, there are interactions between the first and second set of dynamics. Finally, in the later stages of colonial history, the transnational corporation introduces 'invisible' sources of power which may be in conflict with the dominant classes created by earlier colonialism. These new bodies may even have conscripted elements in the colonial population to the service of the new, international system of production.

In attempting to examine liberation movements emerging within such complex processes an analytical key must be found. This may not encompass all of the complexities but may be able to give an understanding of the significant elements of the historical process involved in liberation struggles. Certainly one cannot begin to understand why so many parts of the Third World have tried such different development models; why they evolve in such extraordinarily different ways in terms of political and economic development; one must unlock, with an analytical key, this interaction between social formation as it evolved in the colonial period and the evolution of modern imperialism itself. Therefore three elements which may provide a key to the understanding of the matter are suggested.

First, tactical objectives. As a liberation process begins to form it must be asked: what is the proximate problem that it is trying to overcome; what does it see as the immediate block to its objectives? This is the tactical objective in the sense of the immediate challenge to action.

Secondly, what is the period of history at which the revolutionary process tries to express itself?

And thirdly, there are the strategic objectives. What is the deeper historical accomplishment that is involved? Each of these must be divided into two broad sub-categories looking first at tactical objectives.

A liberation struggle will either be dealing with what it regards as an element of foreign domination, frustration of hopes, aspirations, through foreign control – that is an external tactical objective; or it may be concerned with an internal revolutionary objective, which may result either from one class seeking to replace another or because the masses of a country feel so abused and excluded by the system that they are struggling to break down what they regard as an internal agent of oppression. Therefore, there are two sub-categories – the external and internal blocks to aspiration.

Further, there is the question of the stage of history, and here two periods can be distinguished. One is the early phase of capitalist development, which stretched from the sixteenth century to the late nineteenth century, the time of the emergence of modern monopoly capitalism. This period can be described as covering the formation of capitalism in its dominantly nationalist aspect.

Then, there is the second period. This begins when capitalism ceases to be an exclusively national phenomenon because of the transnational corporation and the growth of finance capital, which together shaped the post-1945 world. We can call that the phase of transnational capital. We will find that revolutionary struggles express themselves in profoundly different ways in accordance with whether they happened in the first phase or the second phase.

Finally, the third category, strategic objectives. All liberation processes must ultimately be concerned with the question: how to nurture productive forces in society which are currently unable to develop either because a backward, historically out of touch ruling class is keeping the society from progressing; or because an external force is frustrating it from moving forward. The first strategic problem is to do with productive forces; how do you get to the point of creating effective productive forces of whatever form?

Our second sub-category of strategic objectives involves social consequences. How can new productive forces be made to work for general justice and not merely replace an old oppression by a new oppression? How can they be made to work for the satisfaction of the needs and aspirations of the people as a whole? This question arises when the nation arrives at a stage where its liberation process releases the capacity to develop an economy within its own control.

Let me summarise the elements of this key. Each

struggle has a tactical objective. The tactical objective can either be the removal of foreign domination or the defeat of an old internal class by a new emergent class. Secondly, a struggle takes place within a specific period in the historical process. It either occurs during the time when national capitalism is developing or when it has consolidated itself and is being transferred into transnational capitalism. Finally, each revolution must have strategic objectives. These can be restricted to the release of native capitalist productive forces or may be extended to include the management of these productive forces to provide the basis for a just society.

This key can be used to analyse a number of revolutionary experiences so that they can be understood within the historical process.

Up to the time of the revolutions of France and the United States, we were dealing with relatively simple phenomena.

Similarly in English history, the struggle led by Cromwell represented an early, almost pre-capitalist class fighting against the control and dominance of a monarchy supported by a landed aristocracy. The country was struggling to emerge from a type of feudalism. The resulting war was an internal conflict because it was the internal aristocracy that was the frustrating agent. This struggle took place in the period of the early formation of capitalism and its objectives were the development of a new type of productive force that was being blocked within the society.

The French Revolution at the end of the eighteenth century was also an internal phenomenon. A growing bourgeois class created by early capitalist formation was straining to break out. It happened in the middle period of capitalist history and its objectives were, very simply, the emergence of a local capitalist force.

The United States of America, created by the New England states, represents a two-pronged struggle. Here, development had reached the point where that society was capable of significant capitalist evolution. But the frustrating agent was external. King George III was a nuisance blocking the process and he had to be dealt with. This occurred in a situation where the capitalist system was maturing historically. The objective of this struggle was the release of native capitalist productive forces. However, the release of these productive forces did not liberate all social groups in American society. For example, the black population remained in slavery until the Civil War in the 1860s. Nonetheless, the American revolution opened the way for the emergence of productive forces which, in turn, laid the basis for the development of American society.

So much for the simple cases! Now comes the period of complexity, that is, all those liberation processes that have fashioned what is now called the Third World.

First a look at the nature of colonialism is required to see if some of the complexities can be understood. Then the exercise can be reduced to certain keys that give an analytical handle on what took place. The first thing to consider is the wide range of societies and internal transformation within societies that are the product of that colonial experience. Consequently, when a liberation struggle commences within one society there may be mixed structures, some of which are still basically feudal; other sections may be pre-feudal; some with incipient modern productive forces of their own; some with incipient capitalist forces implanted by the colonial experience. Thus there may be, in one social formation, feudal and pre-feudal arrangements together with modern productive forces in capitalist ownership. India is one such example.

The second distinguishing feature is the powerful presence of new, landed aristocracies – the latifundistas of Latin America and the plantocrats of the Caribbean – social forces that are created by the peculiar penetration of colonialism.

The third component is what we sometimes call the comprador group – the commercial elements that have been created by the particular exchange relationships; the unequal exchanges of the colonial process. They are responsible for shipping out the primary products and in turn for importing all the things that are part of what we described earlier: that in/out structure of colonialism in which the metropole exports finished goods and draws its raw materials and basic foods from the periphery. The commercial class, therefore, emerges not as a spontaneous product of internal social and economic history, but as the intermediaries of the colonial system. Products of colonialism tend to have divided loyalties and often show little commitment that is patriotic, rooted in their own soil and their own historical experience.

It is inevitable that, because of the kind of production that is allowed as a result of colonialism, the industrial base of society remains small, creating a very small proletariat. Therefore, one of the classic social forces that is the engine of the modern liberation process, the working class, is obviously a very small sector in the social formation. At the same time there is a large peasantry together with a substantial *petit bourgeoisie* made up of professionals, bureaucrats, intellectuals and small businessmen. The latter will tend to be inexperienced, being themselves products of the particular artificial relationships of the system.

It is a fact that liberation movements, like all revolutionary processes, must be fashioned from the social forces in the particular social formation. Colonialism creates complexities and often inserts artificial forms into the local social structure. This accounts for the diverse nature of the national liberation movements and the uneven course they take. For it is no longer as simple as the Netherlands versus Spain; or what the rising French bourgeoisie was doing versus Louis XVI and what he represented; or what Cromwell was fighting for. Here relatively simple social forces were at work. Today, the complexity of the social structures creates unevenness and contradictions in the revolutionary or transformative processes in the Third World.

However, there are some historical oddities. For example, what caused the United States to start what the historians would call a bourgeois democratic revolution in 1776, and why did that produce an extraordinarily dynamic and effective continuity of history thereafter? There is an absolute logic to the way events followed from the original purpose. American society constructed an ideology that was both nationalistic and supportive of what it was doing. Alexander Hamilton stated that they were not going to tolerate the British coming to interfere with areas which he considered American markets. It was now free trade versus monopoly.

If the extraordinary civilisation that has emerged from America is examined closely the question must be asked: why did the seemingly similar revolution of Simon Bolivar in Latin America, which started a bare 33 years later, unfold in dramatically different ways? It cannot be accepted that there was some inherent superiority of the American white by comparison with the Latino. Therefore one is driven to look for understanding at some other aspect of the historical process. Gunder Frank throws light on the matter in his book

World Accumulation 1492–1789 where he looks at the nature of the New England colonisation and the kind of economy that was beginning to emerge. At the time New England did not lend itself to latifundia, did not lend itself to great areas being worked by slaves or peons; but rather lent itself to self-reliant, small farmer activity; to the building of communities in the face of a hostile winter and, out of that beginning, to the development of local village crafts and small industries. In short, the environment demanded the creation of the interstices of a self-reliant economy within the region. Thus one sees how a natural economic phenomenon partly conditioned by soil and the environment helped lay the foundations for the logic with which the development of the capitalist productive forces emerged and were pursued, including that critical element, entrepreneurship.

By contrast it is clear that much of Latin American colonialism was concerned with the development of the latifundia, which in turn created the landed aristocracy which emerged to control the system. The productive apparatus rested upon slave labour of one kind or another, either imported or obtained by the subjugation of the local Indian population. This was also profoundly true of the Caribbean. What do we observe in the liberation struggle in Latin America? It started with what appeared to be a George Washington type of revolution; but in reality it was not. The struggle of Simon Bolivar was essentially a revolution being led by an emerging Latin American landed aristocracy, without a tradition of entrepreneurship and therefore without the beginnings of a tradition which could lead to the development of independent capitalist forces of production. The political key is turned. The political transformation has occurred. But what is the class that dominates the kingdom that has been inherited? It is, in the main, the oligarchy consisting of the land-owners and the merchant class.

Very soon the inheritors began to invite foreign capital to do the job of developing the productive forces. While Alexander Hamilton is saying, 'get thee hence, we don't want you here!', the heirs to Simon Bolivar are inviting the British in. But in no time, the British are overwhelmed by United States economic power. Taking the broad sweep of history, by the time we arrive at the twentieth century, the United States becomes one of the dominant forces in the development of the Latin American economy.

The result was inevitable. In the contemporary period, Latin American societies are very often comprised of weak, locally controlled productive forces with a heavy foreign presence. This is coupled with the attempt to maintain the latifundia as the landed aristocracy tries to hold on to its power. These conditions foster tyranny and corruption. Hence some Latin American nations are not yet evolving in terms of progressive or just forces. Commonly the military (heir to the very armies that removed the Spanish) is utilised as the defender of the class that led it originally, the landed aristocracy of the latifundia. There are many exceptions but there is still a high incidence of this type of stultified liberation process. And it remains instructive to consider how those two revolutions parted company in the way they expressed themselves.

That is why so many Latin American nations have failed to achieve the objective of the development of their own productive forces within their own control and have certainly not even begun to address significantly the problems of just social dispositions within the society as a whole. Hence, there is a new type of revolutionary struggle aimed at liberation beginning to take place in Latin America – until recently in Nicaragua and potentially in Guatemala. In El Salvador the struggle takes the form of a civil war. The productive forces are struggling to be released and harnessed as the basis for a just society. A way is being sought to regain control of the economy so that the productive forces can be essentially native and begin to address some notion of social justice. Not all Latin American countries achieve this by violence. To some extent, countries like Venezuela have attempted this within a pluralistic democratic framework. Similar events are also occurring in Argentina, although it is subject to tremendous pressures. Mexico is an interesting, complex and partly unfulfilled variant in all of this.

The Case of India

India was the first country to win independence in the modern era. When the national liberation struggle began, India was a society that was partly feudal and partly early capitalist. Certainly India had reached a fairly developed productive stage before the intervention of the British Raj which did not completely destroy the existing productive forces. However, a very important distinction is to be drawn between India on the one hand and the Caribbean and Latin America on the other. In the Caribbean the indigenous population, the Arawaks and Caribs, were completely wiped out by the Spanish. In most of Latin America, the Amerindian population was substantially marginalised. What was left was largely the product of the colonial process itself; in the Caribbean, the product of the colonial process exclusively. Not so India.

In India there was an important variant: a country that had a long history of its own, a certain cultural continuity of its own, including importantly religions that were indigenous, different from the religion of the conqueror and therefore resistant to outside influence. India's size was a significant fact that cannot be ignored. These are the elements that give rise to the modalities of the Indian decolonisation process. In 1885 the Congress Party was formed. The Great Mahatma Gandhi began to give it force and direction in 1919 (after his experiences in South Africa). Born out of their own deep sense of history and the cultural implications of the dominant Hindu religion, came Gandhi's 'soul force', the non-violent philosophy. The result was the mobilisation of an entire society in a national liberation struggle aimed at removing the British Raj.

The British tried to compromise in 1935 and transferred certain elements of authority, but they were not willing to accept a fundamental transfer of power and the liberation movement continued under the great slogan, 'India for the Indians', and later, another great slogan, 'Quit India, Britain get out!'. This country was able, out of its own sense of cultural strength and history, to finally achieve political liberation in 1947. The Indian struggle climaxed and removed an external force within one context of the modern phase of transnational capitalism. The objectives of the movement were like those of the United States centuries before: the explicit release of capitalist productive forces. What, therefore, emerged from the Indian experience was the triumph of the Indian bourgeoisie.

Indian history entered a fascinating phase. Nehru, who became the ideological symbol of the national movement of India was himself a socialist. But neither he nor anyone else tried to transform the Congress Party into a socialist party. It remained a party that linked together the national elements – the masses, the peasantry, all the semi-capitalist forces under the leadership of a *petit bourgeoisie* and the intellectuals, and married them to a bourgeoisie waiting to get its chance. This was to produce the India of our time.

And that India is interesting because it has achieved enormous development of its productive resources. From 1947 to the present there has been a vast economic evolution. But, if you look at the total disposition of Indian society, India has still to determine if she can build an internally just and harmonious society on the basis of the productive forces that have developed. There is a sense in which India has reached one point but still has to enter another even more important stage.

The Caribbean Case

Let us now come to the Caribbean and examine Jamaica and Cuba. The Caribbean has to be seen first as the only social formation in modern history that is entirely transplanted. Nobody can trace their ancestry further back than to the point when Columbus stumbled upon us. So that one deals first with this special element in the Caribbean personality, that of the cultural transplant. One of the Caribbean's most talented novelists, V. S. Naipaul, has written compellingly, if cynically, about this phenomenon in his work, *Mimic Men*.

Very important to Caribbean history are slavery and the plantocracy, together with the comprador class and the commercial group which have no rooted loyalty but to the in/out carriage of goods and whose attachments are as much to the external system (which we now call imperialism) as to their own internal society. There is the *petit bourgeoisie* that is profoundly Anglicised (in Jamaica's case). This class is prey to all of that unconscious cultural egocentricity which is typical of the English. The Jamaican *petit bourgeoisie* thought (and to a large extent still thinks) that the Westminster model was the final repository of everything political and that British law was the best that could ever be achieved in history.

Out of all that came three significant points. It is impossible for such a history to have produced an entrepreneurial class. Accordingly, the Caribbean starts with this gaping hole in the armoury of society. There is no traditional entrepreneurial experience, nor even the kind of self-confidence out of which entrepreneurship is born. Secondly, there is a very uncertain sense of nationalism. It is fascinating to look at Jamaican and indeed much of English speaking Caribbean history and note that the first manifestation of the liberation experience was more towards workers fighting for their rights in relation to plantocrats on sugar estates and docks than towards the question of turning the key of political power through political independence. The early nationalist pioneers like Norman Manley in Jamaica spent years struggling to give birth to some ideas of Jamaican nationalism as the fundamental platform on which the liberation process could be based. There was a slow and uncertain shift of focus from just fighting about wages on the sugar estates, to the formation of the early trade union movement, to the point where the society began to comprehend that there were power equations between Britain and Jamaica that had to be altered if the door to anything else was to be opened. Hence there was this strange phenomenon where even nationalism could not be assumed at first. The contrast with India was extreme.

Finally, when in 1938 the modern national liberation process began throughout the English speaking Caribbean it was inevitable that it would be led by its *petit bourgeoisie*, the professional elements who had the training, together with a sense of grievance at being excluded from the best jobs in the colonial bureaucracy. There was also a broad mass discontent spurting from desperate poverty. This meant that sooner or later the working classes with their curious mixture of peasantry and sugar estate labour would become part of the pool of discontent and a liberation movement would emerge.

However, the leadership was comparatively innocent about the nature of the world economy. It was so deeply steeped in the assumptions of British values, British laws, and the British parliamentary system, that it largely failed to grasp the nature of the world economy in which it sought to achieve its freedom. Hence, Jamaica started its liberation movement with the tactical objective of the removal of British political power. However, this took place in the context of the development of the transnational capitalist system in the world economy. The Jamaican struggle committed itself to the objective of releasing its capitalist productive forces. It explicitly wanted to replicate in Jamaica the capitalist form which it assumed from looking at Britain was the viable option. The *petit bourgeoisie* had led the liberation struggle, and it was interesting to see how they operated. They were not responding to the drive of a local capitalistic class trying, like the French or the Americans, to get the chance to release their productive capacity. Rather to address the problem of productive forces they invented a model of dependent capitalism and named it after the location of its first experiment; Puerto Rico.

This was a product of a certain type of Caribbean experience which is, in varying ways, duplicated in Puerto Rico, the Dominican Republic, and elsewhere. Haiti is an exception but could be the subject for a whole series of lectures by itself.

The Puerto Rican model attempted by Muñoz Marín was the model of dependent capitalism *par excellence*. It was predicated on the argument that the Caribbean cannot develop its productive forces without the productive forces of the international capitalist system. It is an explicit, theoretical approach, a deliberate act aimed at building those productive forces. Certainly in the Jamaican case, there was a comparative failure. When Jamaica moved into appendage status between 1962 and 1972 she discovered that foreign capital had no local interest in exploring linkages between one sector of the economy and another, to take but one example. Why should it spend massive sums on research to discover what raw materials can be found locally for a particular industrial process if it can quickly, readily and cheaply get the raw material somewhere else in a system already developed? Hence you were left with the question; how do you develop a national economy if the productive forces are not rooted, first of all, in national soil; driven by your own entrepreneurial resources; your own technology; linking production forward and backward; building the interstices of a truly viable economy? It cannot be done.

So Jamaica found that she was unable to achieve the rapid release of capitalist productive forces or the use of these productive forces as the basis for a just society because there was no adequate local entrepreneurial class, patriotically rooted and committed. Inevitably, by 1972 Jamaica began to learn some lessons.

From 1972 to 1980 the island tried to pull away from the Puerto Rican model of dependent capitalism, struggled to find some path to self-reliance, through encouraging small business and land reform; and by exploring forward and backward linkages. Consequently, it began to accomplish a margin of development of productive forces leading to some possibility of a viable and just society. However, the impetus to self-reliance received a temporary setback when the People's National Party was voted out of office in October 1980.

By that time there was a number of achievements but the world economic structure and the powers that direct it overwhelmed the possibility of advancement in Jamaica. So the country lurched back to a new attempt to reintroduce the Puerto Rican model, pure and simple, despite convincing evidence of the contradictions inherent in that path.

The Cuban Case

Cuba came out of much the same background as Jamaica. In the middle of the nineteenth century Cuba began to be part of the struggle to get rid of foreign domination and Spanish colonialism. It was doing so at a time of transition when transnational capitalism was beginning to form. It then became prey to two things. One is an example of the brutality of an internal tyranny, symbolised by Batista, that made its own experience a nightmare. It also became prey to the power of the United States which intervened in its liberation process and virtually appropriated it.

Simultaneously there was all the obscenity of a Batista along with the excessive and exploitative presence of United States monopoly capitalism. It is inevitable that the liberation struggle which began in the middle of the nineteenth century was incomplete and in need of redefinition by the 1950s. Cuba tried to restructure its liberation process and the struggle in the Sierra Maestra was born leading to the eventual triumph of Fidel Castro and the birth of the modern Cuban revolution.

What is seen in that example? An interesting mixture of factors can be observed. A liberation process can be seen that had to be aimed at both the internal system of the latifundia and external domination, now represented by the formidable power of United States monopoly capitalism in the Cuba of 1959. Therefore the Cuban struggle had to deal with the immediate oppression exerted by the native class which attached itself to United States monopoly capital. This class was led, controlled and directed by Batista himself. It now also had to consider the question of how to address the issues of productive forces and social justice. In the outcome, the liberation forces attempted to finesse and bypass the traditional first stage of revolution which is to release the capitalist productive forces. Instead it proceeded straight to a combination of development of productive forces and social justice through a form of direct socialist economic development.

It is still too early to make a final judgement on this revolution when discussing history in broad sweeps that cover 500 years at a time. But it is already clear that Cuba cannot be dismissed simply as a failure. It has enormous problems and issues that are the subject of profound reservation and difficulty. But it is beginning to develop a set of internal productive forces. Nor is it enough to point out that Cuba receives substantial support from the Soviet Union. Rather one must note that Cuba receives support from the Soviet Union for a variety of historical, diplomatic, geopolitical and military reasons. However, on the basis of that help, it is a fact that Cuba is beginning to build an effective sugar industry, beginning a certain amount of diversification, building large numbers of houses, providing very good schools, beginning now to develop its own mineral industries, its own textile industry. Hence, little by little, within 25 years, one can detect the formation of productive forces. In other words, the Soviet subsidy is being put to work, not disappearing into polo ponies. Nor is it, as in the case of a country like Jamaica, being squandered in a haemorrhage of consumerism which the economy cannot support. Further, when examining Cuba one must note that the country is addressing its social problems, with probably the best educational system in the Third World today, and a very good medical service. With all the problems and the systemic differences seen in the Cuban model, one cannot allow historical vision to be obscured by the tactical requirements of the Cold War. At the very least, Cuba is an experiment in the balance. It remains to be seen what it will do to democratise its system.

The Tanzanian Case

Because it illustrates a different kind of problem, the last example is Tanzania. Here is a society that in 1945 had a social formation in which there were extensive pre-feudal structures, a large peasantry and a small capitalist structure. In this situation the group that threw out the colonial power at the period of transnational capitalism is faced with limited potential for capitalist production. For example, it could not even attempt a Puerto Rican model.

Tanzania attempted to bypass the traditional route to capitalist development and tried to go straight to a combination involving the release of productive forces and building justice in a kind of simultaneous, socialist-cum-social justice development. But Tanzania found that its productive forces were so rudimentary, so unformed in the course of this experience that up to the present it is failing to create an adequate productive base. Profoundly as Nyerere and everything that he stands for is to be admired – in my opinion he is the finest political thinker in today's Africa – the fact is that the Tanzanian experiment is literally hanging on by sheer determination, by political unity, by a high degree of political formation, by the force and example of Mwalimu's own character and leadership and by the fact that he continues to help build a superbly democratic African socialist political process. But in terms of the capacity of Tanzania to begin to achieve the development of its productive resources and all that this implies, it is not getting off the ground.

What is now happening in Tanzania is very instructive. The transnational economic system is slowly crushing Tanzania, hoping to force it into an admission that the only way to develop its productive forces is by having transnational capital come and do it. The Tanzanians are resisting but they do so from a weak economic position.

What conclusion can be drawn? From one point of view, very depressing. But, in the eternal dialectic of history, there is no such thing as a permanent defeat, therefore, depression is an irrelevance. The situation is one in which economic imperialism has essentially internationalised the world economy and has transnationalised power. But now new factors are emerging. One of these is that the imperialist powers of the nineteenth century are no longer the sole focus of control in the world; there is now a bi-polarity to power. Like it or not, the Soviet Union exists and is not dancing to the old tunes. It has its own programme. This means that the items on the world agenda are not set by the old European powers and the United States alone, even though they remain amongst the most important actors on the stage.

The second factor is that out of the transnationalisation of power and the internationalisation of the economy has come something new to the liberation movements themselves. It is the first dawning of an international consciousness of their own. The Non-Aligned Movement, the Organisation of African Unity, CARICOM, Arab Co-operative Structures, Latin American groupings, the Group of 77, all measure the increasing internationalisation of the liberation movements themselves.

The third factor is that globalisation itself has made international action a political necessity.

Finally, the world will either sink into anarchy or develop a rational way to order its affairs. Surely human history has demonstrated that in the long run rational ordering is the choice humanity will make.

4
Theories and Praxis of Development

The first three chapters looked at history. The next three will examine the concept of development from three points of view. First, development from a theoretical point of view. Secondly a discussion of the praxis of development relating specifically to the cases of Cuba, Jamaica and Tanzania. Finally, Third World possibilities for future development, the role of the New International Economic Order (NIEO), the struggle for Third World co-operation, and the major challenges to the political process will be considered.

To discuss the concept of development and the possibilities in today's world it is necessary to know the basis of the present, and in that context examination has been made of the phases in the evolution of the global reality of the present world economic system created essentially between 1500 and 1850.

What constitutes development? Development has two basic elements. First, it has to do with the development of the productive forces. Secondly, it has to do with the harnessing of those forces to build viable societies. The fundamental question however has always been how. There have been two main schools of thought about the notion of development.

The first of these can be called the evolutionary model. This model has its roots in the work of the

66

nineteenth century thinker Herbert Spencer and is developed to a great degree in the work of the great sociologist Max Weber. A major element in this model is the belief that the natural process of society leads towards a growing rationalisation of increasingly complex social arrangements and that this is achieved in stages. This point of view interprets changes and social formations in the world as similar to those that occurred in Europe and the United States.

It therefore leads to the assumption that the Third World must mirror Western Europe and the United States. W. W. Rostow gave this model its economic content in his famous series of lectures titled, 'Stages of Economic Growth: A Non-Communist Manifesto'. Here, the assumptions of growth are capital, entrepreneurship, industrialisation and the mechanisation and chemicalisation of agriculture. The proponents of this model measure growth by gross national product (GNP) and their objective is for the particular Third World country to replicate the metropole.

This can be termed the mirror method. Within this paradigm there are two trends. One is manifested in what is now known as the Puerto Rican model. The other was developed in the 1960s particularly in the Latin American region and is known as the 'developmentalist approach'.

The Puerto Rican model begins by stating that capital for development can only be accumulated by foreign private investment. The model then operates within the framework of 'industrialisation by invitation'. The key tactic used to attract foreign investment is low wages and the promise of a high rate of profit. The strategic objective of the model is rapid capital formation.

The developmentalist approach also begins from the

premise that capital, entrepreneurship and industrialisation are the basis for development.

However, the 'developmentalists' differ from the
advocates of the Puerto Rican model in that their key
tactic is import substitution and a reduction of dependence on foreign trade. Their strategic objective is to
delink from the subordinate position of a peripheral
country and to develop local capital.

Today, the record will show that both these
approaches have failed to produce development as
defined – the significant development of the productive forces as the basis for a just and viable society.

What are the weaknesses in the approaches? In the
developmentalist approach the focus on import substitution tends to concentrate on consumer durables.
This in turn leads to an even more rigid dependence
on imported raw materials, components and spare
parts. It is critical to note that this occurs in a context
of worsening terms of trade. This then leads to
increased pressure on foreign exchange and then logically precipitates a balance of payments crisis. This
leads to dependence on International Monetary Fund
(IMF) adjustment programmes which in turn create
social misery. The strategic concept of delinking therefore flounders on the rock of a global reality and a mistaken notion of development.

In the meantime, the weakness of the 'invitationalist
model' is even more apparent. Capital goes for high
and quick returns in the context of absolute security.
Experience has also shown that foreign capital in many
instances often uses local savings. Because of the need
for maximum security and high returns in this model,
foreign capital tends to invest only to repatriate rapidly.

In many instances capital then uses the very latest
technology and minimises labour content. To achieve

reliable conditions in the political sphere, this model usually relies on authoritarian rule and dictatorships. Taiwan and South Korea are clear examples. The model therefore does not create a just and viable society. Indeed, both trends have tended to widen both the dual society dichotomy and the gap between the rich and the poor.

Both these approaches attempt to ignore the fact that the dominant reality in the world today is the centre–periphery paradigm and that the weaknesses in the periphery were created by the same processes that created the might of the centre and that further, the centre was built through exploitative relationships with the periphery.

Now to the elements of the other model, the 'revolutionary model'. This model assumes, first, that the contradictions of the class alliance which formed the liberation movement have been resolved. Secondly, that the socialist revolutionary process is proceeding under the leadership of one class, the working class, in an alliance with the peasants, intellectuals and in some instances sections of the military. This model has a certain methodology of implementation. Its features are state planning, mass mobilisation and the one-party system. In terms of strategic objectives, it has managed transformation towards goals of mass social justice. However, there are some problems. In the first instance there is a tendency to presuppose a particular political result which may not be objectively possible in a given situation. Secondly, it occurs in an economy that is already locked into a world capitalist system creating enormous problems of dislocation. Thirdly, it usually occurs in the face of enormous pressures from the outside economy controlled by the forces of transnational capitalism. This leads to grave crises which can impede the progress of the revolution. The pressure which Nicaragua was under, and the consequences of that pressure, is a good example. Indeed, more dramatic cases may be Mozambique and Angola.

For the revolutionary approach to work incredible discipline is required particularly during the period of early transition. Given the different political cultures of various territories, it cannot be said that all Third World countries have political systems or cultural traditions capable of adapting to this kind of discipline. And the imposition of this discipline in some instances can lead to distortions that hamper or even destroy liberal democratic forms. Indeed, this difficult problem is sometimes the cause of fundamental differences between those who are in the revolutionary camp.

The first theoretical conclusion about development models is that there are three disabling weaknesses to the mirror approach. The first mistake of this approach is that it does not comprehend the nature of the world capitalist system. The second is that this theory assumes that the circumstances in which Europe and the US achieved the vast changes which occurred between 1500 and 1850 are possible today. For the Third World the time, circumstances and processes are different from what they were for Europe or the US when they began their process of development. Furthermore, it is a catastrophic mistake to think that the Third World today can be expected to mirror Europe and the US when it was the Third World which helped make Europe and the US what they are. Indeed, it is the nature of the world capitalist system, its origins and evolution which created the exploitative paradigm of centre/periphery which lays the basis for today's world. It is a mistake involving ignorance of the historical processes for anyone to believe that the Third World can mirror such a development.

History is not a simplistically linear process. It is a dialectical one. A theory of development for the Third World must begin with the separate stark reality of Third World circumstances and history. It must begin from our reality in terms of our social, political and economic situation. At the same time, it must have an external dimension because social reality is not one-sided but multi-sided and there is an organic relationship between the external and internal processes.

There are two choices. If the political environment is pluralist, hopes lie in a more complete understanding of the difficulties to be overcome in the developmentalist approach. On the other hand, if the environment is revolutionary the external pressures and the initial dislocation which will tend to coincide must be able to be handled. It must also be hoped that the disciplines which can cope with pressure and dislocation do not create their own distortions, to say nothing of the formation of ossified bureaucracy, and a crisis of diminishing freedom.

A theory of development in the Third World must face the challenge of transformation, the transformation of institutions, habits, psychology and skills. One writer, Ian Roxborough, in his *Theories of Underdevelopment* suggests that development can be defined as 'an increase in the capacity for controlled transformation of the social structure'. This is a useful definition and therefore it follows that any development theory that is appropriate for the Third World must involve:

a) the capacity of the social group to agree on goals, that is a political consensus;

b) that such a model must have the capacity to create
    the institutions through which the agreed goals
    may be realised;

c) the development of the productive forces which
    make material well-being available to all, and finally,

d) the creation, through the interaction of a), b), and
    c), of an environment in which people can realise
    their potential for self-expression and self-reliance
    through democratic participation.

In this process there are three critical variables which
the African writer, Archie Mafaji, in his book *Science,
Ideology and Development* identifies. These are ideological commitment, scientific knowledge and organisa-
tional ability. All three are vital to the process of
development in the last quarter of the twentieth
century. For many Third World political activists, the
revolutionary theory is more satisfactory because it
confronts the challenges of transformation. But it can
only arise in special circumstances. For those who are
not in revolutionary situations but in evolutionary
pluralistic situations, the challenge is: how to address
transformation and development?

It is easier to examine the historical process up to the
Second World War since one is dealing with recorded
history. Here one can discern clear outlines of the
nature of modern imperialism and the role of colonialism. However when discussing current development
models one is discussing contemporary experience. In
the long sweep of history there are few accumulated
records of development for post-colonial societies.
Also, the rapid changes which are occurring today
create situations where form may be mistaken for
content. Within the framework of these difficulties,

one must begin by examining the notion of development which is a complex set of factors which determine first, whether a social group is capable of defining a set of objectives for itself, attainable within the political process. Secondly, whether the social group is able to achieve those objectives with increased productive capacity so that a material base can grow as a foundation for social aspirations. Thirdly, whether all of these factors create an enlargement of human experience as people come to contribute more, either because they have jobs or have creative opportunities, or feel that they can influence affairs by the manner in which they participate in the political process. Development is therefore a political process which must define what is being attempted; an economic process which will provide the underpinning; and also look at a socio-psychological process of creating an environment in which people feel enriched and fulfilled.

In the examination of each particular development model, there are some signposts that are worth bearing in mind. They are largely to do with the external and internal contexts within which a development process is attempted, and the first signpost is the geopolitical situation.

The second is the nature and impact of the world economy on the particular developing society.

Thirdly, the nature of the decolonisation process and the struggle for independence, which is often a very profound determinant of what happens.

Fourthly, the class structure of the particular newly independent country when it embarks upon its development path.

Fifthly, in the context of all that, what model should be adopted by whatever political process happens to exist, whether military dictatorship, plural democracy, or revolutionary process.

The geopolitical factor has tremendous significance when talking about the Caribbean, Central or Latin America. The sheer over-arching power of United States hegemony becomes a major factor in any kind of development attempt. In Africa the Frontline States near to South Africa such as Mozambique, Tanzania, Angola and Zambia have geopolitical realities of profound significance. Then there is the special geopolitical relationship that Puerto Rico has with the United States, or the special circumstances of South Korea whose development was influenced by the aftermath of the Korean War. Finally, the immediate geopolitical situation should be placed in the wider context of a world economy that is increasingly dominated by transnational economic power and where a world capitalist system is now highly articulated and supported by critical institutions like the IMF, the World Bank and the General Agreement on Tariffs and Trade (GATT).

The decolonisation process is mentioned because there are fundamental differences that arise from the nature of the independence process itself. Did it come by a series of peaceful evolutionary steps as was common in most of the British Empire? Or was the decolonisation process accomplished by armed struggle (as, for example, in Algeria, Cuba, or parts of Africa) which has a particular set of implication for the development process?

Fourthly, in coming to grips with the peculiarities of development the class structure must be considered because, depending on the nature of the particular colonised society and the type of economic experience it had, there are tremendous differences between, say,

Tanzanian society which did not have a strong, native bourgeoisie when it became independent and Caribbean society where there were highly developed and powerful plantocracies allied to a comprador class, themselves the product of an extended experience of colonisation.

The final factor is the question of models. A great number of countries, including Jamaica for parts of its history, South Korea and most of Latin America, have attempted modifications of mirror development, hoping to replicate the experience of Western capitalism. There are the revolutionary models of which, in the last 20 years, Cuba has been the most famous. In another hemisphere there are the African Socialist models of which Tanzania is the most significant. Then there are those countries that attempt the model of democratic socialism, seeking to pursue the imperatives of fundamental change. In the 1970s Jamaica was part of this band of countries. In terms of the mirror model two countries are important, Puerto Rico and South Korea.

The Puerto Rican experiment sprang from the pragmatic judgement of Governor Muñoz Marín and became celebrated in the scholarly writing of Arthur Lewis. It is sometimes called 'Operation Bootstrap' and also referred to as 'Industrialisation by Invitation'. In essence, the model began with the Rostowan idea of being at a point in history where capital formation is critical. It then concluded that if a country has to achieve the necessary capital formation from within its own internal processes, it may wait forever. Therefore, the key to capital formation is the attraction of foreign capital.

Puerto Rico attempted this model in very favourable circumstances. First, it was proximate to the enormous

United States market and was guaranteed absolute access to that market. Secondly, it adopted a semi-colonial status that was very reassuring to foreign investors. There were many advantages for Puerto Rico including United States federal government expenditure, providing, for example, military services, which can otherwise be a burden on a small, independent state. The status of Puerto Rico was aptly described in the late 1940s by Adolph Bird, as 'independence in everything except economics, defence and foreign relations'.

What are the results of this experience? In 1947 there were 13 United States owned factories in Puerto Rico. By 1967 there were 2,000. In 1948 foreign control of Puerto Rican manufacturing was 22 per cent, and by 1968 it was 77 per cent. During that period a more massive level of foreign investment per square mile of territory took place in Puerto Rico than probably in any other part of the world in contemporary history. Therefore, if the mirror theory is right, with the unusually favourable circumstances which have been described, then logically there should be some indices of accomplishments. However, between 1950 and 1970, some 20 years into the experiment, 615,000 people left Puerto Rico for New York and other cities in the United States. This figure is significant since the Puerto Rican population is less than three million.

It is interesting that with massive injections of capital, classic market opportunities, perfectly controlled environment and circumstances, there is this large export of people. At the same time unemployment rose to 20 per cent and is still admitted to be in the region of 25 per cent although there has been further massive migration since 1970. It is also well known that some 60 per cent of the population still need food stamps to survive.

With due regard to the sincerity of the attempt, the social results of the model are less than impressive, even without discussing the destruction of their agriculture, questions of the Puerto Rican personality, and the development of a national sense of purpose.

South Korea starts with the great advantage of a significant population of 38 million. This is a large base for its internal market and in terms of a standard of living, South Korea could boast of US$1,700 per capita at the start of the 1980s. However, these facts must be qualified by particular factors. The South Korean economic miracle occurred after the Korean War and took place in a context where, when the war was over, there were two confronting entities – North and South, one communist and one capitalist. As was the case after the Second World War when the Marshall Aid programme provided huge injections of capital to shattered Western Europe, so too did South Korea start out with tremendous aid capital from the United States given on very favourable terms. South Korea was now part of a geopolitical reality: an artificial, unique geopolitical reality; a northern showpiece versus a southern showpiece, each side determined to show that it provides the best opportunities.

Secondly, this country is interesting because years of a tightly controlled military dictatorship, together with a union movement that had been tamed, created a situation where the country was enormously attractive to major multinational capital.

Between 1962 and 1979 there was spectacular growth in South Korea where GNP grew by 9.2 per cent per annum. In 1980 there was a contraction of 6 per cent and per capita income moved to $1,700 in 1981; that is, into the middle range. However storm clouds were gathering. South Korea's foreign external debt was $17 billion or 21 per cent of GNP. By 1981 the external debt was $19.6 billion or 32 per cent of GNP. In 1982 it was $77 billion or 60 per cent; and by 1986 it was estimated that the external debt was bigger than GNP.

Tanzania is of profound interest for the study of development for a number of reasons. First, it is the best and most clearly articulated example of what is sometimes termed 'African Socialism'. Some commentators on African affairs have located Julius Nyerere as part of an intellectual continuum which includes Leopold Senghor and Jomo Kenyatta. This is not so. Nyerere represents a significant breakthrough in ideological comprehension because he was the first African Socialist in office to address questions of class formation on the one hand and relations with imperialism on the other. Nkrumah did so in his famous book on neo-colonialism. However this was done while he was in exile. Julius Nyerere attempted to address the question in a profound way by basing his view of socialism on objective analysis and African realities. This approach represents a departure from a kind of romanticism that has enveloped much of African Socialism.

To comprehend the dynamics of Tanzanian society one has to reflect on its history. In this country there are instances of social organisation which were typical of many areas in Africa before the penetration of colonialism. In this situation work, village and land were all part of a communal ownership. Alongside this form of ownership was a reasonably harmonious social existence. To a certain degree this history was marked by the breaking up of the former structure and a period of war-like monarchies that emerged in its history. In 1914 it became a German protectorate and thereafter increasingly integrated at a very simple level into the colonialism/imperialism matrix. Its sisal plantations were developed as well as its cotton and similar products. Soon it became a classic example of those land areas that are used to provide simple basic commodities for the metropole.

At the time of decolonisation, there was neither a significant local bourgeoisie nor a significant local plantocracy nor native comprador class. It was also dominated by peasants and a *petit bourgeoisie*.

During the decolonisation process there was no armed struggle because the British colonialists were skilful at that type of strategic, constitutional withdrawal which leaves essential economic control in foreign hands.

It is also interesting to look at the nationalist leadership of this process in Tanzania. Julius Nyerere is essentially an intellectual, a teacher from the *petit bourgeoisie*. In 1964 Tanganyika and Zanzibar united to form the nation state known as Tanzania. Between 1964 and 1967 attempts were made to develop using traditional methods. It was felt that foreign capital would deal with the problem of industrial development. Further, the economic ties with traditional partners in the imperialist system were maintained because that was logical and the main emphasis at the start was directed toward Africanisation and the building of political institutions.

However, by 1967 certain things became clear. Foreign capital did not appear to any great extent and when it did show, it wanted to obtain management contracts. There was little inclination to risk massive doses of capital in Tanzania. As a consequence externally owned capital formation did not occur. Looking at the experience with its traditional trading partners

Tanzania realised that the implications of these relations, the terms of trade and the balance of payments,
were not favourable. It appeared to the leadership that
when the imported tractors cost more, and the sisal
fetches less and when shipping charges mysteriously
escalate, it becomes time to think afresh. This led to
one of the most significant intellectual developments
in modern politics – the rethinking of African
Socialism by the Tanzanians under Julius Nyerere's
leadership, the clear articulation and proclamation of
the idea of self-reliance. All of this became encom-
passed within the famous *Arusha Declaration* of 1967
which in turn led to a series of strategies of which the
most famous was the idea of the Ujaama Village.

What Nyerere has said and written emerged from a
profoundly humanist idea about the development of his
people and how they could participate democratically in
the processes of development. It began with a clear state-
ment and reversed much of the traditional thinking on
development which sees industrialisation as the classic
instrument of the process. He stated: 'Industrialisation is
not and cannot be a priority for Tanzania. There is not
the money with which to finance it, there is not the
means and therefore it cannot be.'

That is a very significant intellectual departure. But
more followed. Nyerere went on: 'In our circumstances
money cannot be the key to development.'

Instead he said development has to be achieved by
concentrating on agriculture. He also provided a definition of the concept of development as being all
levels of people participation and the establishment of
genuine democratic institutions. Nyerere stated: 'There
is no freedom without development. There is no development without freedom.'

It was clear that the Tanzanians were determined to prevent the appearance of new classes that would oppress the population. To this end the *Arusha Declaration*'s posture towards political leadership was strict. Among other things it advocated modesty and limitation of private property rights for politicians. Its aim was to curtail the growth of the *petit bourgeoisie* using its access to the state to become all powerful.

Therefore Tanzania started with a wide programme of nationalisation of banks, trading firms, mills, sisal estates and most of the major industries. They also attempted a significant reorientation of education and tried to develop the concept of the Ujaama Village as the focus of an agricultural co-operative model which would achieve rural transformation. It was hoped to reconnect the Tanzanians to their earlier experience where villages and communities were automatic, communal co-operatives.

What are the results of this attempt? It is fashionable today to speak of the failure of the Tanzanian model. It is true that over this period Tanzania has only achieved roughly two per cent per annum growth in GNP. It is true that in 1984 Tanzania's per capita national income was $280 per annum with a population of 19 million. Certainly therefore by GNP tests there has not been any significant expansion of the economic base. However, it must be remembered that Julius Nyerere said from the start that his country would not be able to accomplish that kind of development quickly. Nonetheless, in terms of the quality of life, there are some things which are worth looking at. The illiteracy rate has been reduced from 90 per cent to 21 per cent in the period. The number of doctors per head of population has not changed much – it was one for 18,000; it is now one for 17,000 in spite of a

3.4 per cent population growth. Nurses show a better picture – one to 12,000 when they began, now one to 2,900.

What conclusions can be drawn from this? First, to say that no development has occurred would be one-sided. Secondly, it is clear that while the economic base has not improved dramatically, the post-independence quality of life has improved. The problem however is a complex one. There is not an automatic connection between economic growth and an improvement in the quality of life – a question for discussion at a later stage.

Democratic Socialism in Jamaica

In 1962 Jamaica became politically independent. For over 300 years the island was ruled by British coloni-alism. As a consequence the structure of the island's economy, based upon the plantation model, was a skewed one. The country produced commodities and raw materials for export, in particular, bauxite, sugar and bananas. However, it continued to import its basic essentials and many of the components necessary for the production of the above commodities. It was a legacy from the days of the plantation state.

Eight years after achieving political independence and in a period where there was consistent growth in the gross national product fuelled by the expansion of bauxite and tourism, the Jamaican economy did not adequately satisfy the needs of the majority popula-tion. Unemployment continued to be high, social con-ditions were abysmal as many districts both in urban and rural areas did not have water or electrical facilities. At the same time, the economic policy pursued by the government meant that the economy, while growing, was dominated by foreign capital. Studies done at that time showed that in the manufacturing sector 75 per cent was owned by foreign capital, financial institutions were 64 per cent owned and tourism was 58 per cent foreign owned. The mineral industry was 100 per cent controlled by multinational corporations. By 1972, 70 per cent of the Jamaican economy was foreign dominated.

It was within this context that the People's National Party assumed office in February 1972. The new PNP government had four major objectives:

1. To create an economy that would be more independent of foreign control and responsive to the needs of the majority of Jamaicans.

2. To develop an egalitarian society both in terms of opportunity and in terms of the value of people.

3. To develop a more democratic society.

4. To accelerate the process by which Jamaicans could recognise their history.

Between 1972 and 1974, the People's National Party government sought to institute social changes which would reflect these objectives. In particular, there was the establishment of the National Youth Service, the lowering of the voting age to 18, the repeal of the Masters and Servants Law, a literacy programme, and the establishment of a national minimum wage. In 1974, however, the price of oil rose. The impact of this was deleterious on the Jamaican economy. At the same time, the government had begun to talk to the bauxite companies about re-negotiating the operations of the mineral companies. These negotiations did not proceed without acrimony and in the end the government had to impose by law in Parliament the Bauxite Levy. The negotiations with the bauxite companies commanded wide support across all classes in Jamaica. The government had sought to increase Jamaica's share of the benefits of the industry. Perhaps, however, it was the PNP's redeclaration of socialism and the beginning of ideological debate in society which triggered a process in Jamaica. The redefinition of democratic socialism in the 1970s caused internal polarisation within the Party. At the public level, more radical pronouncements set in train deep fears. In a real sense, society was unprepared for this ideological debate. However, the Party and the government needed a political philosophy to guide them in achieving the four objectives.

Recognising this, the Party embarked upon an immediate programme of political education. However, this programme was not consistent or sustained. By 1979, the difficulties triggered by the ideological debate were resolved and the Party embraced a document called *Principles and Objectives of the People's National Party*. This document speaks to the essence of democratic socialism and the operational methodology for its achievement.

In the economic sphere, the result of the government's policy was that foreign domination of the economy was reduced to 47 per cent and particularly in the agricultural area, the government established sugar workers' co-operatives on former plantations and developed a land lease programme which distributed land to small farmers. Continuing its programme of social reform, the government instituted free tuition at the university, worker participation in industry, established community councils as a way of democratising community life, established maternity leave with pay for women and instituted by law the compulsory recognition of trade unions. All these things obviously had a profound impact upon society. The attempt by the government to deal with the internal questions of social engineering and the rhetoric of socialism disturbed the old oligarchy.

As part of the policy of democratic socialism, the government began to pursue an independent and non-aligned foreign policy, part of which was recognition of Cuba. In the 1970s, South African troops invaded Angola. The Angolan government requested the assistance of Cuban troops to repel the South Africans. The issue became a major international one. Jamaica, which has a long history of support for the anti-apartheid struggle dating back to the early 1960s, took the position that Cuban troops invited by the Angolan government were legitimate. This obviously incensed elements in the United States administration. From that moment relations with the United States became increasingly strained. By 1976 the Jamaican economy began to feel the effects of the rise in oil prices and the down-turn in the world economy. However, the Jamaican people voted in December 1976 to continue support for the government. For the next four years the country went through a difficult period. The attempt by the government to deal with internal questions of social justice led to the 'revolt' of the bourgeoisie. The attempt to articulate a foreign policy that was based on a concept of non-alignment and involved Jamaica dealing with Cuba became a point of great controversy in relations with the United States.

The idea that the hegemonic reality means that a small country must do what the big power instructs requires rejection. There cannot be a Non-Aligned Movement if it cannot contain within its ranks everything from the utterly pro-United States Saudi Arabia to the pro-Soviet Cuba. If members of the Non-Aligned Movement who emerged from the decolonisation process are removed on the grounds that one country is too pro-West or one is too pro-East, the Non-Aligned Movement would soon consist of about three little countries with a minuscule population.

In 1972–80 the government of Jamaica was concerned to build regional structures, to give Third World countries a little more strength and to build inter-cultural structures between the English speaking Caribbean and Latin America. The Caribbean and Cuba are a part of that matrix. The United States was of course very hostile to the process and the Jamaican upper classes were angry about social justice. All these factors came together resulting in a contraction in the economy. The People's National Party was crushingly defeated in 1980 and the process of self-reliant development was set back.

In 1980 those who believed in the mirror theory of capitalist development were returned to office. The new government came to power on the promise of tremendous support from President Reagan who declared that Jamaica was going to be a model for the world. The whole model was an absolute reversal of the democratic socialist experiment and the government began to divest all the things that had been brought under public ownership. There was also deregulation of the apparatus of a socially directed economy and a return to the free market economy with the IMF 'cheering' in the background. Finally, there was the return to absolute dependence on foreign capital.

For seven years the 'magic' of a 'pure free market' experiment was given every opportunity. What were the results? Unemployment has remained at around 23 per cent.

The island's gross domestic product (GDP) in 1987 is the same as it was in 1978. There has also been a reduction in per capita income of 12 per cent. There have been decreases in output in the sectors of mining, manufacturing and construction. As regards foreign debt, the situation is acute. In 1980, the island's external debt stood at US$1.86 million and the ratio of debt to foreign exchange earnings was 130 per cent. In 1987, this ratio had increased to 250 per cent, and debt servicing consumed over 42 per cent of the national budget compared to 21 per cent in 1980. The 'magic' of a pure free market system led to disastrous results. In February 1989 the Jamaican electorate pronounced judgement on this model of development when the Jamaica Labour Party was defeated in general elections.

5
The Struggle for Change: The New International Economic Order

The question of the environment – that world economy which is the structure within which Third World countries try to develop – starts and ends this publication. Today three crucial factors can be identified which impact on Third World countries. The first is the structure of the world economy. The second is the steps which Third World countries must take to gain strength by their methods of co-operation with each other. Thirdly, how individual developing countries might devise internal strategies that can cope with development in the sense of producing more wealth while transforming oppressive structures into viable societies based on both effectiveness and justice.

Let us start with the world economy. The entire discussion of the current external environment of the world economy and its relationship to the Third World needs to be set in a context of urgency because of the crises mounting at every level. There are some interesting indices of elements of the problem. For example, take the debt crisis which exercises the minds of all sides at this time. In 1973 Third World countries were requiring some 12.6 per cent of the value of their exports to finance debt – that is interest and sinking fund. Today this stands at 32.5 per cent of gross export earnings. In the case of Jamaica, over 40 per cent of all export earnings is being used to service external debt. Even member states of OPEC, the Organisation of Oil Exporting Countries, which showed a 12.2 per cent average in 1973 are showing a 19.1 per cent average now as the value of their energy exports stagnates, the cost of money rises, and the terms of trade move against them.

A number of objective causes make the crisis even worse than before. The terms of trade are continuing to move against commodity exporters; another is interest rates which are maintained at their astronomical levels. Those interest rates can be directly traced to internal policies in the United States to do with taxation, military expenditure and the budget deficit. Then, there is the drive towards protectionism which continues to be a factor. All these elements are combining in a concrete sense to exacerbate the present situation.

At the same time there is the economic and moral crisis illustrated in just one grim example in 1984; Ethiopia and its famine.

In the European community, the cereal surplus was some 3.7 million tons – the community decided to send 35,000 tons to help millions of people who were dying. The United States harvest was 70 million tons and 80,000 tons were allocated to go to Ethiopia.

In 1980, one in four of the world's population ate too little to be healthy; one in 73 was dying from malnutrition; in that year alone, 12 million children died because of protein deficiency. Meantime, the First World observed that its own conditions were less than ideal. The growth rates of 1973 which ran at 6.3 per cent were minus 0.2 per cent in 1982; unemployment rose among First World countries from an average of

3.4 per cent to 8 per cent in 1982. Even the inflation rate of 7 per cent in 1973, in the interest of which the great deflationary policies have been pursued and the massive unemployment accumulated, remained at the same rate until the late 1980s.

In this context what is the New International Economic Order (NIEO) and the struggle for change about? The idea of a number of important reforms in the world economy and the way it operates actually had its roots in the Non-Aligned Movement and can be traced to attitudes and declarations in the famous Bandung Conference of 1955 which launched the Movement. By 1973 the Algiers Summit began to give precise expression to NIEO prescriptions in the Action Program for economic change. In 1974 this was adopted by the Sixth Special Session of the United Nations and in November of that year the 29th General Assembly voted in the majority for what was called 'The Charter of Economic Rights and Duties of States'. In the course of all this, the United Nations Conference on Trade and Development (UNCTAD)* was developing as the main arena in which the discussion about the world economy took place. Around the same time the Third World began to evolve an identifiable body in the world community known as the Group of 77 which coordinated Third World efforts in the economic field within the UN system.

The four main planks on which the NIEO proposals rest are trade, industry, finance and the multinational system.

On trade let us look at the experience of Jamaica which is typical of Third World countries everywhere. In 1962 (the year of Jamaica's independence) 20 tons of sugar could supply the means for the purchase of

* See Appendix for explanation.

one tractor. By the 1980s the same tractor required 60 tons. This is the story of the terms of trade, the negative position of the commodity exporter. In looking at that problem, the advocates of the NIEO formulated a specific response known as the Common Fund. This Fund proposed, firstly, to identify 18 major items in the world commodity trade, for example sugar, bauxite, cotton and copper, recognising that because of the international division of labour created by colonialism, the Third World is heavily dependent on these products. The Fund proposed to take these items and create a body for the general management of the exchange of those commodities in the following steps:

1. The Fund would be created first by the contributions of different countries in the international community which was later to be supported by a levy on the price at which these items were traded. In this way there would be a continuing basis of finance. These funds would then be used for two basic purposes, as follows:

   (a) if the market price was falling badly, the Fund would be able to intervene, buy the product and maintain the price. This would have the effect of eliminating those terrible valleys in earnings which wreak havoc with the capacities of a small country not only to finance itself, but even to plan its development,

   (b) by the same token, and quite reasonably, in times of shortage where tremendous commodity price peaks exist, stocks would be able to be unloaded thereby generally stabilising the product.

The obvious advantage would be to create predictability in earnings for Third World countries. It would provide trigger mechanisms for both the buying and the unloading of stocks so that, by international agreement, manageable parameters are maintained.

Where the base and ceiling are placed would be the subject of negotiation from time to time. If the general experience of the price movements of manufactured and capital goods and the products of heavy industry showed a chronic tendency to move upwards over say, five years, (which is the nature of the crisis of the adverse terms of trade) the Fund would be able to adjust the minimum and maximum trigger mechanisms. This would create a broad concordance between average commodity prices and average industrial product prices, and the result would be not of some theoretical intervention in advance, but based on the actual experience of what was happening.

2. Where particular Third World countries, heavily dependent on a commodity, experience some natural disaster such as flood or drought, and suffer a sudden and great loss of foreign exchange earnings there would be a scheme of compensatory financing. In this way some of the shortfall of foreign exchange would be made up during the crisis permitting the country to maintain the management of its affairs in a reasonable way.

3. Finally, there would be special 'second window' operations available to Third World commodity producers for research and assistance in product diversification. The entire mechanism therefore was designed to create stability, buoyancy and a capacity for development within the whole process of commodity production.

No one is pretending that the Common Fund could have solved the world's problems. However, there is no question that it could make a tremendous contribution to the capacity of the Third World to relate to the world economy of which it is a part in a just and manageable way. It is interesting that the idea of providing a special basis on which the determination and support for the exchange between raw materials and agricultural products on the one hand, and manufactured and processed goods on the other, is 100 years old. The whole existence of European agriculture rests upon a carefully worked out set of political arrangements that ensures that the farmer, say within France, does not fall behind as a lost victim of French economic development. So, within national boundaries nobody has the slightest problem introducing intelligent political management aimed at just and equitable results in a major part of the economy even if the economy itself is supposedly capitalist and supposedly devoted to the principles of free enterprise. Common sense enjoins this kind of effort and even in the Lomé Convention* there are echoes of this kind of arrangement. For example, there is a compensatory financing scheme for primary producers who may run into disastrous harvests.

Nothing in the Common Fund is revolutionary, extraordinary or without precedent. But, when it was advanced internationally as distinct from nationally or even within a historical association such as the Lomé Convention, it ran into an absolute storm of First World resistance.

In the end, the idea of what was called the 'integrated programme' had been whittled down by First World opposition. By that time, what remained for discussion was a very limited and emasculated version in which there were eight commodities which were

* See Appendix for explanation.

accepted by the First World; each to have a mini Common Fund by itself. There was to be no capacity for cross subsidy, protection or management. The idea of a source of funds for research purposes was blown away; and even the idea of creating a concordance between the levels of the trigger mechanism and the movement of say, tractor prices, had been discarded. However, even on this absolutely reduced scale, there was a crisis because many First World countries would not agree to put up the modest sums of money for the particular commodities that would be necessary to get the whole process started.

In 1978, in Runaway Bay, Jamaica, a conference was held to break the deadlock. The participants were Helmut Schmidt of West Germany, Pierre Trudeau of Canada, Malcolm Fraser of Australia, General Olijeyu Obasanjo of Nigeria, and Carlos Andres Perez of Venezuela. President Jimmy Carter was invited to attend but could not. A number of items were raised and cleared. West Germany and Canada changed their positions on the Common Fund and the conference got to the point where the whole programme was passed in principle. This was confirmed in UNCTAD in Geneva in 1979 and then it went to Washington. The United States was the final holdout against the question: how much money should be voted to actually start the very limited operation contemplated? In the end, Washington wasn't willing to agree so the whole plan was stalled.

In industry the story can be told very simply. In the 1970s the Third World contributed about seven per cent to the world's industrial production. Having regard to the fact that they make up approximately two-thirds of mankind they set themselves the modest target of trying to reach 25 per cent of the world's industrial production by the year 2000. The notion rested on two ideas – one that there should be a liberalisation of the general system of preference so that if the manufactured goods of say, South Korea, were beginning to be a threat, they would no longer promptly be blocked by protectionism. The second feature was to try to set up a system of international funding so that there could be compensatory financing to help with the problem of relocation of labour and industry, where the natural competitive working of the system might cause difficulty.

Some politicians state that they are against the NIEO because it interferes with the workings of the free enterprise system. Yet, when South Korea produces at lower cost something that is being produced in Scandinavia or in the United States which is a free enterprise economy in its classic sense, the very countries which will resist the idea of the NIEO are the first to raise the walls of protectionism against the workings of free enterprise to protect their own threatened industries. The Third World, knowing that this is so, thought of the idea of the compensatory financing arrangement to help with relocation, so that there would not be unnecessary social dislocation. That idea was stillborn; it did not even get as far as a mini conference like the one in Runaway Bay.

The next thrust of the NIEO is monetary reform. One aspect of this must be isolated and a sensitivity to the problem of foreign exchange crisis in a Third World country must be held. Traditionally this precipitates an IMF intervention followed by social crisis, followed by further economic crisis, followed by further IMF intervention, followed by further political crisis followed by the cycle that seems to go on forever.

It is strange to think that even in the 1990s the world is incapable of managing money intelligently. Human society invented money for one simple reason and that was to facilitate economic activity.

The IMF emerged as part of the Bretton Woods Agreement after the Second World War. It was introduced because of the determination of the developed countries to avoid the trade wars and protectionism of the 1930s. The IMF was established to provide a reserve fund to assist a particular country which might have run into a foreign exchange shortage while it was still in the process of trying to become competitive with its exports. Rather than witnessing economic wars, it was to be a rational mechanism for dealing with the problem.

The methodology was, first: if a country ran into foreign exchange difficulty it would go to the IMF. The Fund would then require that a planned devaluation of the country's currency be carried out. The devaluation would have the effect of making imports more expensive and exports more competitive, and theoretically put a brake on imports and stimulate exports. Secondly, this had to be supported by a programme of internal money management on the theory that if you contract the internal money market then the producer who has been accustomed to providing for the local market cannot sell. If he is to maintain his rate of profit he must now look to export. Meantime, the devaluation makes him competitive once again and so, theoretically, he is able to maintain his level of profits. The contraction of the internal market is the 'stick'; the more competitive export prices are the 'carrot'.

To achieve the internal contraction of money, there has to be a reduction in budget expenditure and a freezing of wages. The social costs of both are considerable.

Theoretically, it is understandable that an economy which exhibits highly developed aspects of production (that is to say there are factories and a farming community that know how to produce effectively, who understand efficiency and the latest technology) may benefit from such a programme. If that kind of economy gets into trouble because it becomes uncompetitive in terms of international trade, one can understand the demand management methodology of the IMF working because the problem in its factories, for example, may be expressed in the number of shifts of highly trained workers that are laid off; the highly skilled management that is underemployed; the supervision that is on short time and so on. Thus, if the devaluation and other measures make exports attractive, there are sales teams that know the world market, know how to get out there and move. There are trained workers who can put the swing shift and later the graveyard shift back in operation. There will be an agricultural community that knows how to plough the land once more, move in the fertilisers, pesticides, chemicals, and deliver the products to the point of distribution. The economy should have the capacity to respond to the medicine and most important, that economy will also have a general welfare safety net so that when human suffering results in the short run, because of the adjustments of the programme, there is assistance for the people.

When that methodology was applied in 1977 to a Third World country like Jamaica, two serious problems arose. First, Third World economies by definition are not highly sophisticated with reserve capacity waiting like a caged lion to be released; there are few farmers who are straining to unleash their inherent productivity. Most likely the country's economy is based on agriculture which is still largely peasant, and where often the problem is how to get the farmer to understand the methodology of modern production. In other words, there is not a massive proletariat all geared up for production.

Problem number two is that the very poverty and underdevelopment of the society probably means there is no significant welfare net. Contraction erodes further this fragile social net and in the end leads to acute social dislocation. So Third World conditions are different. However, the IMF will say that you must make these changes within a three year adjustment programme under watchful IMF eyes. The time scale of the programme ensures that the country cannot develop the factors of production that could take advantage of the export opportunities within the period.

So the result is that in applying a type of First World medicine designed within a mature capitalist system for its own purposes, to a completely alien Third World situation, the IMF creates conditions where massive increases in the cost of goods of essential consumption are visited on a population very often already at the margin of survival. No wonder, therefore, that IMF prescriptions were followed by riots in Egypt, disaster in Peru and social upheaval all over the world with governments being hurled out of office.

The question might well be asked: why does the Third World country accept it? Why not reject it? The reason is simple. The IMF exercises massive influence over the attitude and the behaviour of the entire international banking system by what is called the IMF 'seal of approval'. The IMF itself does not have much money to lend to countries troubled with balance of payments problems. But its seal of approval, in theory, triggers a positive response from the world banking community which then lends funds to the country so that it can get through its crisis. If the IMF does not give its approval it is unlikely that the international commercial banking system will treat the particular country favourably. That country may then find that its choices are between a period of very acute suffering and shortages through foreign exchange difficulty, or finally bowing to the IMF's terms.

To deal with this situation effectively the Third World has proposed, quite simply, that the IMF should modify its approach as the world's reserve banker in the light of the reality of the Third World experience and situation. The first change that is necessary is that adjustment programmes be put in a longer time frame so that struggling economies have time to plan and take advantage of whatever the adjustment programme provides. Secondly, that there should be far more funds available so as to put a genuine supply of 'oxygen' into the system. Thirdly, and this is most crucial, that the world should understand that the Third World's problem is not primarily one of adjustment, but one of development; not primarily one of putting a second shift to work but one of building the new factory; not primarily one of enabling the farmer to exploit export opportunities but of trying to get him to be an effective producer in the first place.

An understanding of the reality of the Third World reveals not just the futility but the cruelty of the present IMF prescription. What is needed is either a brand new institution that deals with the problem of development finance and development foreign exchange support, or a window in the IMF that has a completely different perspective on these problems. No one is asking that a corruptly run Third World country which takes most foreign aid to support the

polo ponies of the rich should receive aid irrespective
of its final destination. On the other hand, the policies
of the IMF, which right now are completely dominated
by the United States and the OECD group of countries,
are largely irrelevant to the needs of poor countries
because the decision making process is not influenced
by a Third World perspective.

The fourth area involves transnational corporations
and here the NIEO has sought to introduce a Code of
Conduct. This would require transnational corporations to consult with and advise host governments of
changes in plans and operations which might affect a
country significantly.

Jamaica had an experience with the Reynolds Metal
Company which operated in Jamaica for over 30 years
mining bauxite for processing into alumina and aluminium in the United States. Reynolds discovered that
the nature of the world aluminium industry had
changed due to enormous increases in the cost of
energy. It was more economical to shift to other parts
of the United States rather than to work out of the old
east coast and southern basin aluminium plants.
Reynolds simply ceased the Jamaican bauxite mining
operation without notice to the government. They
destroyed revenue expectations, dislocated workers and
their families, and upset the aspirations of entire communities. This is regarded as the right of the multinational corporation, no matter what profit has been
made out of the exploitation of a resource for years.
The Code of Conduct would require some sort of prin-
cipled behaviour regarding the giving of notice and the
holding of negotiations with host governments. The
Code of Conduct was agreed by the United Nations
system but collapsed in Washington because the proposed enabling legislation was blocked by the US; they

agreed with the Code but didn't agree to any legislation in support of the agreement which they felt was contrary to the principles of free enterprise.

When examining all the elements of the NIEO and the progress that has been made one sees a stalled process. It is now in a cul-de-sac, and the next stage is vital since the survival of millions of Third World people is at stake.

The external component necessary to the strategies of development – South/South dialogue and co-operation between developing countries – must now be examined. This is the untried element in what Third World countries can hope to do to ensure that political independence is not absolutely contradicted by economic reality. To be able to develop internally and alone is impossible in today's world. Therefore, any act of national development must reflect the interaction between internal and external events.

The whole theory of South/South co-operation arises partly from the idea of delinkage and the need to reduce dependence on the old metropolitan links. This has given rise to a number of regional bodies like the Central American Common Market, the Caribbean Community and Free Trade Area, and the East African Common Market to name a few. However, these have to be viewed as a number of specific components. For example, the Caribbean Community provides the territories with a bigger market, and a larger area for an exchange of goods as a basis for production. That is a step forward.

The more important part of the procedure is how to build an integrated economic process between the different units. Very often people think of this as just meaning trade with each other. That is the most superficial side with a more significant aspect being the integration process. That deals with the provision of services such as shipping within the region which each territory would be financially too weak to attempt alone. Jamaica in the 1970s made common arrangements with Colombia, Cuba, Guyana, Mexico, and Venezuela and formed a regional shipping line which was commonly owned. This meant that some part of the trade of the region was now creating surplus that remained at home instead of adding to the coffers of the international shipping magnates.

Even more important than the common services are attempts to find the means to build incremental productive capacity through joint inter-regional planning. Here are two examples. One was the proposal by the late, great Dr Eric Williams, who, in 1975-6 proposed that the Caribbean should establish a Caribbean Food Plan. This would consider the use of idle lands in different parts of the Caribbean and utilise the strengths existing in the various areas. For example, Jamaica, which is good in a number of agricultural areas, could provide manpower, while Trinidad's oil industry would supply down-stream products like fertilisers and chemicals of various sorts. The idea was to pull together a number of factors of production within the region and direct that effort to greater self-sufficiency in food. This would engage resources, reduce dependency, increase nutrition, increase employment and generally create the beginnings of that foundation of agricultural change which is supposed, in the classic theory, to precede attempts at industrialisation. That was a correct idea.

Another example was attempted in Jamaica with the bauxite industry. At one stage the whole operation was owned and controlled by multinational corporations. This meant that no matter what Jamaica tried, the decision-making process was in the hands of those corporations.

Nonetheless the question arose: is there any room for incremental production? Surveys of the world markets showed that the Mexican economy was growing and getting to the point where it was becoming an aluminium consumer; in the Middle East more sophisticated economies were also beginning to need aluminium. Most importantly, investigation showed that the Soviet Union had the second largest aluminium market in the world and also the fastest growing and most reliable market because of the nature of their planning processes. Jamaica, together with the Mexicans and later the Algerians and the Iraqis, decided to market the product themselves. Instead of getting into those markets by a further increase in multinational corporation production, it was decided to create the incremental capacity by national effort. This idea was rational, full of common sense and completely devoid of rhetoric.

Jamaica had its tremendous reserves of high quality bauxite; Mexico had its gas as a source of cheap energy; Algeria and Iraq had the same. There was a potential market. It was challenging and exciting. The group had to design a productive complex, find the technology, finance, and negotiate supply contracts. Planners from Iraq, Algiers, and Moscow looked at points of entry for the products. Finally, a highly viable scheme was confirmed to be very sound by top US feasibility consultants. Part Hungarian and part American technology was to be used and it was to be financed through funds mobilised by a British finance corporation. An American firm which had worked in Jamaica, Kaiser Aluminium, was going to be the supervising contractor and the markets were in place.

It was looking good in 1979. Then, the Iran/Iraq war blew the scheme out of the water. The first casualty of that war was what would have been a most dramatic and effective example of South/South co-operation.

In summary, South/South co-operation is vital in its own right. The NIEO is completely stalled because the decision makers of the First World have no interest in even a modest reform of the way the world economy works. Therefore, one is thrown back upon the ability of the Third World countries to attempt that extraordinarily difficult process of some degree of development from within their own resources and in the presence of a hostile environment.

Development and Internal Transformation

Looking at development in this hostile international environment there are many cases of genuine, Western style democracies which are operating with plural political institutions and enjoying the rule of law and incorruptible judicial processes. However, they may be drifting deeper into various problems which are ameliorated just sufficiently to keep the whole thing from falling apart.

It would be useless to discuss further the controlled capitalist experiments. If a country has a dynamic trade union movement, it cannot be wished away in order that a South Korea can be created in another Third World country. South Korea may be an economic miracle from one point of view but it is a guided form of capitalist experiment. It is idle to talk about that as a general development model because the process began in very special circumstances. Accordingly, argument will be directed towards those

Third World countries struggling for development within a framework of plural democracy.

So far the results have been poor. Within this framework countries are faced with two options. They can decide to go the purely foreign capital route where foreign capital is seen as the only engine of development. If that is done then there is a replication of the problems with which the Third World is historically beset. Therefore the model which rests upon foreign capital alone is incapable of providing real development.

If on the other hand the country is going to experiment with some kind of development model that is based on internal capital formation supplemented with doses of foreign capital, it then runs into a series of contradictions. Experience shows that as a country moves towards internal capital accumulation, it may run foul of the immediate problems of workers at already low standards who have a natural and proper desire to be paid more. If it tries to contract the returns on capital to the owners and otherwise tries to support an egalitarian movement forward in the society, it faces the crisis of a revolt of the capitalist or entrepreneurial class along with the associated problems of flights of capital, of skills and a general non-cooperation in the system. This then develops into a foreign exchange crisis which leads back to the IMF crisis, then into the crisis of reversal and, finally, the country is required to pursue the other path to be able to survive. It can become a vicious circle. Very often it is at this point that military interventions and dictatorships emerge. It is felt that one of the problems is to be found in a fatal disjuncture within the system between the nature of the economic process which is demanded and the manner in which the political system works.

All of the classic politics of the Western democratic model is based on the assumption that the political process has nothing to do with the economic process except at best to regulate it – to ameliorate what it does; that the business of the political process is twofold. One is to hold out some programme of promises that get people to vote, the other is to then hopefully keep those promises or make the people forget that they were made. An examination of the workings of the political process in Britain, Germany, France, the United States or even Jamaica, demonstrates that there is almost no aspect of political activity that addresses the questions: how can an economy be structured to move forward if it is to be both incremental and just? What is demanded of the worker, the manager, the entrepreneur? How can these social groups fit within a broad matrix of national purpose and what is the contribution each must make to this success? What must each do, if success is to be possible? Nowhere does the political system direct the mind to process and struggle but only to result and benefit. That is the nature and the heart of the system.

Therefore, within one limited part of the equation, it is clear that, if the internal development process is to have any chance of handling the problem, then the fatal disjuncture between the process itself and the rest of social reality must be closed. That is not just rhetoric.

If the political process is seen not so much as organising people to vote around promises, but rather to mobilise people for particular tasks; if it is conceived in terms of profound political education; if it is directed towards the raising of the understanding of social reality and historical process rather than an appetite for the products of the system; if political work and rhetoric can be directed to dealing with realities, then there is hope.

For example, a country must learn to survive forgoing the luxury products of some other country as efforts are made to create an opportunity for initial agricultural development. Positive attitudes to co-operative development which make land reform a viable proposition in the long run must be formed. This is better than condemning it to a minifundist disaster as terrible as the plantation system which preceded it.

How can this be achieved? Should the multinational corporations run the country? Or should the old oligarchies do the job? Certainly, merely to reform and divide the land is impractical. The little farms that are inefficient will take the country no further. On the other hand, there is a way in which a country can transform rural areas to create social gains within the context of incremental economic gains and that is through some form of co-operative movement. But this movement rests on high levels of consciousness, high levels of discipline, high levels of training. The present political process in traditional Third World democracies does not deal with matters of this sort.

How therefore to build a juncture so that political, social and economic processes are one unfolding unity is a great internal challenge. Where that kind of challenge is met, there is more chance of being able to deal with South/South co-operation.

Coming back finally to the NIEO. Even if South/South co-operation is possible, and it begins to improve the capacity for internal transformative development through a local political process, there is still the problem of the hostile environment. How is that environment going to change?

One of the reasons it is unlikely to be changed is to be found within the political processes of the First World. France is a most recent example. François Mitterand

and his Socialist Party came to power the first time in May 1981 with a strong programme for transformation. But as soon as the Mitterand government went into action, the entrepreneurial class went into rebellion. In no time Mitterand faced a flight of capital out of France into Zurich and other parts of Europe. Such is the nature of the nation state that, although the majority of people were going to suffer, other European countries were glad to receive the capital. In no time the French government was thrown into catastrophic reverse. They were obliged to dismantle the entire programme of change. What followed was not easily distinguishable from the programmes of Giscard d'Estaing.

What caused that? Two things. First, the populist nature of any European political process, and two, the way in which the nation state acts to continue to divide the people so that they cannot reach a general understanding of a common problem.

Capital is now completely international in perspective, with an international agenda and a long term view of its own interests. Countries are national and therefore short in perspective and encouraged by their political processes to the short term view of their own interests. What is needed therefore, is a series of developments. These have to begin in the Third World itself in terms of its own political processes. It must begin with a supporting political perception of why co-operation between Third World countries can provide that wider matrix without which the effort is impossible. That means being willing to raise the consciousness of people, being willing to experiment with new forms of mobilising people while remaining perfectly democratic and subject to elections.

Sooner or later the First World must come to some point when the inevitability of that chronic 10 per cent unemployment in Britain, and the 6 per cent unemployment in the US are challenged. What is it in the structure that continues to condemn them? One day the minority groups must begin to question, as Jesse Jackson has invited them to do, the system and look beyond the horizons of traditional patterns. It is going to rest upon the capacity of social democracy to be a vanguard within the First World to develop a matching political process, to learn to have programmes of common action in Europe that do not leave a Mitterand isolated when he tries to move. The majorities within each developed country will have to learn the secret of transnational political action if transnational corporations are to be accountable once more.

The Socialist International is working to develop these mechanisms and processes. The survival and development of the world is going to depend on peace movements realising that their main problem is not the problem of arms, but a deeper problem of how the world is organised and to what purpose. Even feminist movements must understand that what they fight against with male chauvinists is replicated over and over in the way the world itself is arranged.

If all of that can begin to happen internally and externally, the beginnings of transformation of the Third World and indeed of the wider world might be seen.

6
Agenda for Change

At all points of history political activity takes place within the context of the economic conditions which the productive forces shape. This is not to say that politics cannot affect economics. Political action may delay or accelerate the evolution of the productive forces. Certainly, political action can help to shape the social consequences which flow from these forces but in the end it is economics which dictate the ground rules.

As the end of the twentieth century approaches the dominant reality of the world economy is the increasing globalisation of production. National boundaries previously defined the areas within which groups of people pursued their economic activities. Now the cumulative effect of technology in every area of human activity is creating a situation in which national boundaries merely delimit the platforms of production. The dispersal of different elements of the productive, distributive and financial sections of the economic chain is acting to reduce the capacity of any one nation to affect or even significantly influence the outcome of economic activity. As a consequence the concept of the nation state as an arena for independent economic development is becoming increasingly obsolete.

However, the globalisation of the world economy has not led to a more equitable distribution of wealth but is facilitating its further concentration. It has not brought Third World countries into the power centres of the international division of labour, but has left them as marginalised as before and less able to affect their peripheral status by political action.

Meantime the concept of change is central to politics and political strategy. All processes of change involve three elements. First, change towards what and to what end; secondly, the means to change; and finally, the forces that are likely to oppose. In a world where so many people are poor; so many are malnourished and without hope, the case for change is irresistible in ethics and supported by common sense.

In the perspective of a small, energetic Third World country like Jamaica the case for change begins with the internal condition of continuing inequality and the social malformation which it reflects. At the same time change in the sense of better living conditions for the majority of people is bound up with the capacity to achieve sustained economic growth. Furthermore, growth must directly involve increasing numbers of people in some aspect of economic activity. However, it becomes more and more apparent that any strategy of economic development, social distribution and popular empowerment is bound up in the nature of the world economy and the location of developing countries within it. Accordingly, the extent and nature of internal change possible is increasingly determined by the evolution of the global economy toward interdependence.

The first consequence of globalisation is that delinking as a possible path for economic development for Third World countries is more remote than ever. In the 1970s, many Third World countries sought to develop economic models with the objective of securing economic independence.

The essence of these models was the fact that since the commanding heights of the economy, in many cases, were controlled by the former colonial power, then an essential ingredient of economic independence was the nationalisation of these commanding heights and the delinking from what was the Western capitalist system.

In the 1970s, in particular, many Third World countries engaged in this model of development.

In the 1980s economic realities plus stagnation in many of these countries resulted in a shift away from these economic policies to integration in the world capitalist system. This shift was made under the impact of globalisation and the consequential reduction in the objective strength of the nation state.

The inexorable logic which flows from this reality is that economic survival is related to larger rather than smaller economic aggregates. Europe responds to this with its Common Market for 1992 as do the United States and Canada with their Free Trade Act. Equally each developing country must look to its regional neighbourhood for an equivalent opportunity to combine its economic planning and productive rationalisation. In a very simple sense the greater economies of scale which regional co-operation make possible are at the very heart of the challenge facing developing countries. It is for this reason that the agenda of the 1990s essentially differs from that of the 1970s by being more concerned with the empowerment of the South rather than with pleading with the North.

Therefore the agenda for change has to begin with South/South co-operation but it must also include the reform of the multilateral institutions to ensure that some means of international mediation remains possible. South/South co-operation is the platform from which developing countries must seek to define for themselves their location within the world economy. Simultaneously, to ensure their survival and increased effectiveness, the multilateral institutions must be reformed and this service the Third World can provide for mankind as a whole. It is these institutions which provide structures within which developed and developing nations can seek to negotiate to reconcile their interests. Furthermore, the world's populations will learn in due course that it is only through international political institutions that people will have any means of affecting the direction of economic activity and more importantly, the consequences for humankind.

From every point of view it is important to co-operate with the farsighted leadership of the North in demonstrating the self-evident truth that its own long term interests coincide with those of the South to the extent that the economic expansion of both is a pre-condition of international stability and the best guarantee of sustained growth of the North itself.

In summary, reshaping international economic relations and the reform of multinational financial institutions continue to be key elements for an agenda of change in the 1990s. However, in a world where ethical pleas fall on deaf ears, the South has no option but to guard its own fences and create its own opportunities.

Meantime, three problems occupy centre stage in contemporary experience, one new and two as old as history. The new problem is debt. Third World debt has become the hangman's noose, strangling the hope of orderly economic expansion. The world needs to address this problem if social expectations are to be fulfilled.

The old problems involve the position of women in society and the condition of the environment in the world. No agenda for change can ignore these two issues. Women constitute more than half of the world's population and continue to represent, with few local exceptions, the most disadvantaged group in human history. By their own energy and directed by an increasing consciousness women represent a constituency of interest which cannot be ignored. In countries like Jamaica, women are becoming the best scholars and the most able and dedicated administrators, yet they continue to suffer disadvantages in terms of the law and in economic opportunity.

Problems of the environment go back as far as the droughts and famines of Ancient Egypt when Joseph of the many coats taught the Pharaohs to anticipate with timely storing of excess production in times of plenty.

Then there are the dust bowls which wrecked parts of the United States in the 1930s and are creating havoc in the more northerly regions of Sub-Saharan Africa. The Brazilian jungle in relation to the ecological balance has become a *cause célèbre*. In reality, if humanity does not take global charge of the maintenance of the environmental balance it faces crises of unimaginable proportions.

As with the physical environment, so too with the physiological. Drugs and the huge international criminal structure which produces, processes and markets them represent an item on the agenda no less important because it is so macabre. Once again the collective human will is challenged to respond.

And so far as the political agenda is concerned, in spite of changes which have occurred recently in South Africa, and in spite of the heroic struggles of the

ANC and other organisations in South Africa, the system of apartheid is still not yet buried.

Apartheid and its end therefore still command the attention of the world. Like the problem of debt, both tarnish the landscape of the world political order. These are some of the essential questions on the agenda of change for the 1990s.

Then there is the eternal question of democracy. This is a moment in history where the idea of popular choice and involvement is in the ascendancy. *Glasnost* and *perestroika* in the Soviet Union, the recent revolutions in Eastern Europe demonstrate the universal aspirations of humankind. In Latin America the democratic process is taking root. Perhaps it is this drive for democracy which is expressing itself not just in electoral practices but in the deep desire of people to participate in the shaping of their lives that is the beacon of hope for humankind. At the same time the struggle for democracy has added to a concept of development. Gross domestic product (GDP), provides an important precondition for positive change but it is not the only measure of development nor the only appropriate focus for national effort. In the end no social activity can claim validity unless it contributes directly or indirectly to an improvement in the quality of life for all people, and in particular for those currently left behind. Equally, economic growth that does not incorporate proportionately more of the people warps social ethics and may increase social instability.

Any realistic vision of change must be based on the notion of empowerment of people. The agenda for change must seek to facilitate that empowerment. In the final analysis humankind must develop economic and social institutions which are just in purpose and democratic in form. Otherwise the world will stumble from one disaster to the next. The agenda for change, therefore, is not invented by visionaries in search of some unattainable new society. Rather, it is rooted in the need for survival and must be shaped by participation even as it opens the doors of opportunity wider.

Appendix

Bretton Woods

This is the name of the international conference which was held at Bretton Woods, New Hampshire in the US in July 1944. The Conference discussed post-war economic problems. The agreement of the Conference resulted in the establishment of the International Monetary Fund (IMF) and the International Bank for Reconstruction and Development (IBRD).

IBRD (World Bank)

The role of this Bank is to encourage capital investment for development projects in the developing countries. It also plays a central role in coordinating aid policy amongst donor countries.

GATT

The General Agreement on Tariffs and Trade. Operating since 1948, it is committed to the expansion of multilateral trade and encourages the reduction of barriers to free trade. Over 80 countries are signatories to this agreement.

IMF

The International Monetary Fund. Established as part of the Bretton Woods agreement in 1944. The IMF was established to encourage international co-operation relating to monetary matters. In the 1970s, increases in the price of oil placed acute strain on the balance of

payments of many third world countries. This led
many of these countries into IMF agreement. Today,
there is a great controversy around the character of
IMF agreements. Many Third World countries agree
that IMF programmes do not take into consideration
the nature and structure of underdeveloped
economies.

UNCTAD

United Nations Conference on Trade and Development. First developed in 1964 to discuss global trading
issues. Since that period its conferences have sought to
elaborate positives on world trade. Its meetings are
used by Third World countries to negotiate positions
in the interest of the South.

Lomé Convention

A convention signed in 1975 at Lomé, the capital of
Togo, by the members of the European Economic
Community and 46 developing countries in Africa, the
Caribbean and the Pacific (ACP States). It replaced pre-
vious association agreements made by the original six
members of the EEC with former colonies (Yaoundé
Convention) and the East African Community (Arusha
Agreement). The East African Community is a
Common Market of Uganda, Kenya and Tanzania.
Under the Lomé Convention all ACP industrial
exports, and most agricultural exports, to the EEC are
free of duty. Financial and technical aid was also
agreed upon and the European Development Fund was
set up by the EEC to administer and channel aid funds
to the Lomé countries.

Bibliography

Many of the ideas developed in this book were stimulated by my reading of a number of authors. They are listed here both so that the reader can further pursue these ideas as well as an acknowledgement.

M. Manley

Samir Amin, *Imperialism and Unequal Development*, Monthly Review Press, NY, 1977.

Samir Amin, *Accumulation on a World Scale*, Vols. 1 & 2, Monthly Review Press, NY, 1974.

Paul Baran, *The Political Economy of Growth*, Monthly Review Inc., USA, 1957.

George Beckford, *Persistent Poverty*, Oxford University Press, London, 1972.

M. Barrett-Brown, *The Economies of Imperialism*, Penguin Books, London, 1974.

K. Brutents, *National Liberation Revolution Today*, Vols. 1 & 2, Progress Publishers, Moscow, 1977.

Dennis Cohen and John Daniel, *Political Economy of Africa*, Longman, Essex, UK, 1981.

Fitzroy Ambursley and Robin Cohen, *Crisis in the Caribbean*, Heinemann, London, 1983.

Andre Gunder Frank, *Capitalism and Underdevelopment in Latin America*, Monthly Review Press, NY, 1969.

Andre Gunder Frank, *Dependent Accumulation and Underdevelopment*, Macmillan Press, London, 1978.

H. Goulbourne, *Politics and State in the Third World*, Macmillan Press, London, 1979.

Herman Girvan, Richard Bernal, and Wesley Hughes, 'IMF and Jamaica', *Development Dialogue* No. 2, 1980.

Teresa Hayter, *The Creation of World Poverty*, Pluto Press Ltd, London, 1981.

Ankie M.M. Hoogvelt, *The Third World in Global Development*, Macmillan Press Ltd, London, 1982.

J.H. Hobson, *Imperialism*, University of Michigan, Ann Arbor Paperbacks, 1965.

Nigel Harris, *Of Bread and Guns*, Penguin Books Ltd, Harmondsworth, England, 1983.

A.S. Kenwood, *The Growth of the International Economy 1820–1980*, George Allen & Unwin Ltd, London, 1983.

V.I. Lenin, *Imperialism, The Highest Stage of Capitalism*, Progress Publishers, Moscow, 1977.

Arthur Lewis, *Economic Survey 1919–1939*, George Allen & Unwin Ltd, London, 1949.

Harry Mogdoff, *Imperialism*, Monthly Review Press, NY, 1978.

A. Mafeje, *Science, Ideology and Development*, African Publishing Company, New York, 1978.

Carmelo Mesa-Logo, *The Economy of Socialist Cuba*, University of New Mexico Press, USA, 1980.

Julius K. Nyerere, *Freedom and Development: A Selection of Writings and Speeches 1968–1973*, Oxford University Press, Nairobi, 1974.

Dan Nabudere, *Political Economy of Imperialism*, Zed Press, London, 1977.

Walter Rodney, *How Europe Underdeveloped Africa*, Bogle-L'Ouverture Publications, London, 1972.

A. Philips, 'The Concept of Development', *Review of African Political Economy* No. 8, 1972.

Rius, *Cuba for Beginners*, Writers and Readers Publishing Cooperative, London, 1980.

Justirian Rweyemamu, *Underdevelopment and Industrialization in Tanzania*, East Africa Publishing House, Nairobi, 1973.

Issa S. Shivji, *Class Struggles in Tanzania*, Heinemann, London, 1976.

Eric Williams, *Capitalism and Slavery*, Capricorn Books Editions, New York, 1966.

Documents

Documents of the First Congress of the Communist Party of Cuba, Progress Publishers, Moscow, 1976.

Principles and Objectives of the PNP, People's National Party, Kingston, 1978.

The Arusha Declaration, published by Tanzanian African National Union, Tanzania, 1967.

Index